Beyond The Fear Lenormand Oracle: Understanding Negative Lenormand Cards

English Edition – 2025 © by Liz Figueroa Lenormand.

ISBN:979-8-218-59743-6

Registered by *Safe Creative* on 16 January 2025 Reg. No. 2501160646414

Credits:
Design and content by @2025 Elizabeth Figueroa-Vazquez (Liz Figueroa Lenormand). Editing and formatting for print and digital distribution done using Canva

For inquiries, comments, or additional information, you can contact the Autor at: lizfigueroa2012@gmail.com

Note: This is the official English translation *of Cartas Negativas: Oráculo Lenormand.* The original Spanish edition published in 2025.

Beyond The Fear Lenormand Oracle

Understanding Negative Lenormand Cards

By Liz Figueroa Lenormand

Dedication

To my dear students of the past, present, and future, whose curiosity, questions, and eagerness to learn have been the driving force behind my passion for teaching. The information shared here is my way of thanking you: for every Zoom conversation, affectionately dubbed "our henhouse," moments filled with laughter, shared anxieties, and a constant learning of Lenormand that brought us together as a community and elevated our knowledge to a more personal level.

Each conversation sparked new practices and perspectives, deepening our understanding of the Lenormand oracle.

For this and so much more, I thank you deeply with all my heart.

With affection,
Liz

Index

"Opportunities gallop toward those ready to take the reins."

Note: Image created by Liz Figueroa using AI

Prologue

The Negative Cards and Me

Since I began teaching Lenormand in 2014, something has caught my attention: the complex relationship few of us have with certain cards, especially the "negative" ones. I will not lie—at first, I avoided them myself. It was easy to ignore, set them aside, or try to disguise their messages with "positive" interpretations that, if I am honest, did not always make sense. I did it with the best intentions, but I soon realized that this habit affected my accuracy as a reader. I was not being precise or genuine, leading me to deep reflection.

Why did these cards make me so uncomfortable? Was it their symbolism? Was my personal history interfering with my readings? I realized that the only way to improve was to face my fears and see these cards from a broader perspective, not just as warnings but as learning tools. I had to work on my relationship with these cards, understanding them from their traditional roots and on a more personal and spiritual level. I asked myself: how can I interpret these cards authentically without letting my issues contaminate them? After all, those seeking a reading deserve clarity, not a reflection of my insecurities.

This personal reflection led me to question not only my methods but also the traditional approach that often underestimates the transformative potential of these cards. This project was born from that moment: an exploration to understand negative cards beyond their apparent harshness and recognize them as key components for deep and balanced readings.

This book, part of my teachings, was my first step toward that mission. In it, you will find theory and practical tools that will help you transform your perspective on these cards. With this introduction, I invite you to dive into the content. From the challenges we face when interpreting these cards to the strategies that turn them into allies, this material has been designed to guide you to more apparent, precise, and meaningful readings. Let us get to the cards!

Liz Figueroa
LENORMAND

www.LizFigueroaLenormand.com

What is the Lenormand Oracle?

The Lenormand Oracle is known as a traditional card-reading system that has enchanted seekers of insight for centuries. An oracle known for its practicality and directness, Lenormand readings often provide clear answers to specific questions, making them a favored tool for guidance and decision-making. Unlike Tarot, which consists of 78 cards divided into Major and Minor Arcana, the Lenormand deck consists of only 36 cards. Each card depicts a simple image of a singular subject, numbered and often featuring a playing card insert. The Lenormand oracle originated in Germany in the 1790, redesigned and named after the famous seer Mlle. Lenormand, few years after her passing.

This oracle has transmuted and traveled around the world, gaining unique adaptations. In Latin America, particularly Brazil, it is expansively known as "Gypsy cards" or Brazilian Lenormand, where the cards are associated with Orishas deities and varied meanings. Moreover, Lenormand has evolved with geography, language, and cultural perceptions, offering diverse interpretations across regions.

It is imperative to understand that the Lenormand oracle is not a subset or variation of the Tarot. Terms like "Tarot Lenormand" can be misleading, as both systems are fundamentally different in their meanings, structures, and methods of interpretation. While the Tarot delves into psychological and spiritual themes, often employing archetypal imagery, the Lenormand focuses on practical, straightforward messages through combinations of simpler symbols. Keeping these concepts distinct is crucial to avoid confusion and respect each system's unique essence.

STRUCTURE OF A LENORMAND CARD

Fig. 1 *Steampunk Lenormand* by Liz Figueroa

How is Lenormand Interpreted?

Lenormand readings are rooted in patterns and combinations rather than single-card interpretations. Here are the core principles:

- **Cards Work in Pairs or Groups:** Unlike Tarot, where single cards often stand alone, Lenormand relies on the interaction between cards. For example, "Clouds + Sun" signifies confusion resolving into clarity.
- **Direct and Practical Meanings:** Each card has straightforward meanings that can adapt to various contexts (e.g., love, work, health).
- **Contextual Interpretation:** The surrounding cards heavily influence the meaning of any given card. Lenormand readings are like forming sentences where every card contributes to the overall message.
- **Questions Matter:** A well-phrased question helps to frame the reading, ensuring accurate and relevant guidance.

Fig. 2 Combining from different directions

Common Lenormand Spreads

Lenormand readings can range from simple two-card spreads to intricate layouts like the Grand Tableau. Below are examples of popular Lenormand spreads:

1. The Two-Card Spread
   - Purpose: Quick insights and clarifications.
   - Example: Card 1 (situation) + Card 2 (description).

2. The Three-Card Spread
   - Purpose: A concise overview of the past, present, and future.
   - Example: Card 1 (past) + Card 2 (present) + Card 3 (future).

3. The Five-Card Spread
   - Purpose: A deeper exploration of a situation or question.
   - Structure: Card 1 (past) + Card 2 (present) + Card 3 (center focus or main message) + Card 4 (near future) + Card 5 (outcome).

4. The Nine-Card Spread
   - Purpose: Detailed exploration of a question or theme.
   - Structure: A 3x3 grid where the central card sets the focus, and surrounding cards add depth.

5. The Grand Tableau
   - Purpose: A comprehensive view of all areas of life.
   - Structure: This spread uses all 36 cards in a grid format. It provides insights into multiple areas, such as relationships, careers, and future potential.

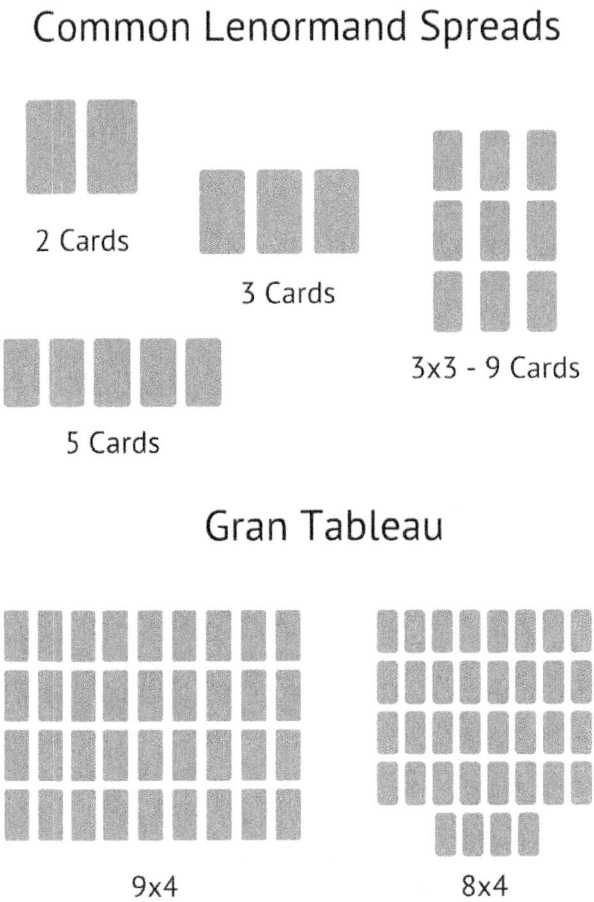

Fig.3 Different styles of spreads

Purpose of This Book

Although we can explore much more about the Lenormand oracle, this book will focus on nine particular cards of a negative nature. These cards often pose interpretive challenges for Lenormand students, creating fear or apathy that can hinder their readings. By addressing these cards specifically, we aim to help readers develop their understanding and move beyond these obstacles.

Basic or Traditional Meanings of Negative Lenormand Cards

- Clouds: Confusion, doubts, temporary worries.
- Snake: Manipulation, setbacks, or detours.
- Coffin: Endings, closures.
- Scythe: Drastic cuts, abrupt decisions.
- Whip: Arguments, repetitions.
- Fox: Deception, pretense.
- Mountain: Obstacles, distance.
- Mice: Theft, loss, decay.
- Cross: Suffering, pain, faith.

Traditional Meanings of Lenormand Cards

Below is a concise reference guide to the traditional meanings of the 36 Lenormand cards:

1. Rider: News, movement, arrival.
2. Clover: Luck, opportunity, small blessings.
3. Ship: Travel, exploration, commerce.
4. House: Home, family, stability.
5. Tree: Health, growth, longevity.
6. Clouds: Confusion, doubt, uncertainty.
7. Snake: Deception, strategy, complications.
8. Coffin: Endings, transformation, loss.
9. Bouquet: Happiness, beauty, gift.
10. Scythe: Decisions, danger, sudden change.
11. Whip: Conflict, repetition, discipline.
12. Birds: Communication, stress, discussions.
13. Child: New beginnings, innocence, potential.
14. Fox: Cunning, strategy, work.
15. Bear: Authority, strength, finances.
16. Star: Hope, guidance, goals.
17. Stork: Change, improvement, transition.
18. Dog: Loyalty, friendship, trust.
19. Tower: Institutions, isolation, perspective.
20. Garden: Community, social life, events.
21. Mountain: Obstacles, challenges, delays.
22. Path: Choices, decisions, alternatives.
23. Mice: Loss, deterioration, stress.
24. Heart: Love, passion, relationships.
25. Ring: Commitment, agreements, contracts.
26. Book: Secrets, knowledge, study.
27. Letter: Communication, documents, messages.
28. Man: Male figure, querent, or partner.
29. Woman: Female figure, querent, or partner.

30. Lily: Peace, harmony, maturity.
31. Sun: Success, positivity, clarity.
32. Moon: Emotions, creativity, recognition.
33. Key: Solutions, revelations, certainty.
34. Fish: Finances, abundance, flow.
35. Anchor: Stability, perseverance, security.
36. Cross: Burdens, faith, destiny.

Your Journey with Negative Lenormand Cards

- If you could describe your current relationship with negative Lenormand cards in one word, what would it be? (Example: Challenging, Inspiring, Mysterious, Transformative, Overwhelming, etc.)

- What is the biggest insight or lesson you hope to gain from working with negative Lenormand cards? (Write your response below in one or two sentences.)

NEGATIVE LENORMAND CARDS: CHALLENGES, LESSONS, AND NEW PERSPECTIVES

Through my experience as a Lenormand instructor, I have noticed an undeniable challenge when addressing the topic of negative cards. These challenges do not stem from me as a teacher but from the students' perception, whether due to personal reasons, geographical aspects, language, or simply the association with Tarot cards. Explaining this topic on many occasions feels like walking on a path of broken glass, where the slightest imbalance in my explanation could trigger chaos of more questions or, worse yet, more fear.

Part of this phenomenon can also be attributed to the lack of Lenormand information available in Spanish today and the resistance of some students to see the cards beyond their traditional meanings. Do not get me wrong: when studying Lenormand, it is crucial to establish a solid foundation from a conventional point of view. However, we must also remain flexible in our observations and adapt to each specific topic, using the information available with discernment.

In traditional Lenormand, the negative cards are Clouds, Snake, Coffin, Scythe, Whip, Fox, Mountain, Mice, and Cross. These cards may bring bad news or heavy energy. However, mostly contain a glimmer of positive potential behind their evident negativity, even when not paired with other cards.

EXAMPLE OF INTERPRETATION: THE CLOUDS AND THE MOUNTAIN

A stormy cloud represents the Clouds card, while on the other side of this cloud, a radiant sun appears as if to say that after the storm comes calm. This symbolism may seem hopeful, but traditionally, the Clouds represent doubts, worries, and even states of depression. A reading of "The Clouds" often reflects confusion and the inability to see clearly. However, it can also show that difficulties are temporary and that a resolution is within reach if one can overcome the moment of uncertainty.

On the other hand, we have the Mountain card. At first glance, this card depicts a mountainous landscape that might invite you to climb and discover what lies beyond or make you accept its imposing height and the distance it represents. Traditionally, the Mountain symbolizes significant obstacles, barriers, or blockages, especially when interpreted within a reading focused on movements or goals.

However, this card can also be observed as an invitation to perseverance. Mountains may seem insurmountable, but they also offer a privileged view to those who decide to face them with determination. In this sense, the Mountain reminds us that obstacles are opportunities to grow and strengthen our character.

PERSONAL INFLUENCES VS. REALITY

What makes a card "negative"? On many occasions, I notice an immediate adverse reaction to negative cards based on the reader's personal experiences—for instance, the appearance of the Snake card. Many Tarot enthusiasts might associate this card with Death or the Devil. In most cases, the reader loses their focus and gives way to personal experiences of betrayal, seeing the Snake only as the lover, the other woman, or even a mother-in-law. In reality, during the original question or in combination with adjacent cards, this card may not even be relevant to the context of the reading.

It can lead to several scenarios: a complete deviation from the purpose of the reading toward the reader's personal experiences or the creation of unfounded fears for the querent. This is why I always emphasize the importance of the reader's cleansing so they can overcome their own negative experiences and provide more accurate and constructive interpretations.

THE CARDS BEYOND THEIR TRADITIONAL MEANINGS

One of the most significant limitations for a Lenormand student is seeing the cards beyond their traditional or basic meanings. This lack of vision may lead to these cards being overlooked in reading simply due to ignorance, personal bias, or a lack of abstract perspective. However, we are surrounded by symbolism in our daily lives.

Take, for example, "The Cross" card. To someone unfamiliar with Lenormand, this card might be associated with cemeteries, churches, religion, or even hospitals. For a Lenormand reader, however, the Cross
indicates suffering, hardship, or total loss. In the context of love, it can point to emotionally burdened or karmic relationships that require effort. Work might signify heavy responsibilities, a challenging workplace, or a project that demands sacrifices.

WHAT HAPPENS WHEN POSITIVE CARDS SURROUND A NEGATIVE CARD?

As in real life, moments of calm and happiness come after every problematic event. This also applies to negative cards surrounded by positive ones. The positive polarity of some cards tends to soften the adverse tendencies of Lenormand's negative cards.

For Example:

Cross + Sun: Release of a burden, sacrifices that are worthwhile.
Mountain + Clover: Temporary obstacles or quick resolution.
Scythe + Mice + Sun: Here, we could interpret:

- ***Option 1:*** A sudden or drastic theft, which, with the Sun, turns out to be beneficial or profitable for those who committed it.
- ***Option 2*:** Despite theft, there was a resolution or possible recovery of what was lost.

PRACTICAL TIPS FOR HANDLING NEGATIVE CARDS

- Perform personal and spiritual cleansing before advising others with the cards.
- Keep an open and flexible mind.
- Consider the overall context of the spread.
- Use clear questions and simple language to guide the interpretation.
- Always communicate with tact and empathy.

Reflecting on Negative Lenormand Cards

1. Which of the negative Lenormand cards in a reading predicted an event that came true? (Write the card name(s) and briefly describe the event if you would like.)

2. Have you moved past the memory of that event, or does it still influence your Lenormand readings? Choose one:

   - I have moved past it and now view the card objectively.
   - The memory still lingers, influencing my interpretations.
   - Other: ____________

MEDITATIVE REFLECTION

~ CONNECTING WITH NEGATIVE CARDS ~

The negative cards of Lenormand hold a remarkable power to dive into the depths of our emotions, unveiling fears, doubts, and the hidden, uncomfortable aspects of our lives. But these cards are far more than messengers of challenges—they are gateways to self-discovery and transformation. Each one invites you to confront your inner shadows, offering the opportunity to grow stronger, wiser, and more resilient. They light the path to personal empowerment, showing you how to turn adversity into triumph.

In this section, you'll embark on an illuminating journey through a thoughtfully crafted questionnaire that will deepen your relationship with these cards. This isn't just a list of questions—it's an invitation to uncover the emotional blocks and patterns that shape your readings. By reflecting on each question, you'll gain profound insights into how your perceptions shape your connection with the Lenormand deck. This is your chance to unlock the wisdom hidden within your emotional responses and transform your readings into a tool of clarity and empowerment.

Additionally, you'll explore a meditative guide designed to strengthen your bond with the negative cards. This isn't just a practical exercise—it's a soothing journey of healing and self-discovery. As you work through the meditation, you'll release fears and misconceptions, replacing resistance with acceptance and understanding. It's a comforting process, a chance to rediscover the transformative magic of Lenormand and embrace its lessons with an open heart and renewed confidence.

SELF-DISCOVERY QUESTIONNAIRE

Take a moment to answer the following questions honestly. Write down your responses to deepen your personal understanding:

What emotions do negative cards evoke when they appear in a spread?

- Fear
- Confusion
- Rejection
- Curiosity
- Other: ____________

Do any of these cards (e.g., Coffin, Mice, Cross) remind you of a difficult or painful experience in your life?

- Yes (write about the experience): ____________
- No

Do you tend to interpret these cards only from a negative perspective?

- Yes
- No

What personal beliefs do you have about challenges and losses in your life?

- I see them as opportunities for growth.
- I struggle to accept them.
- Other: ____________

What do you hope to learn by working with negative cards?

- Acceptance
- Strength

- Positive perspective
- Other: ____________

CARD-BY-CARD REFLECTION

THE CLOUDS

When you see the Clouds in a spread, what emotions arise in you?

- Confusion
- Unease
- Hope (bright side)
- Other: ____________

In what area of your life do you feel there is uncertainty or lack of clarity?

- Work
- Relationships
- Personal decisions
- Other: ____________

What do you usually do when you feel confusion in your life?

If the Clouds were a metaphor for a current challenge, what do you think lies beyond the storm?

- Resolution
- Peace
- Progress
- Other: ____________

What positive symbol or image could you associate with the Clouds to transform them into something hopeful?

THE SNAKE

What impression do you have of the ***Snake*** when you see it in a reading?

- Distrust
- Admiration (for its cleverness)
- Fear
- Other: ____________

Is there someone in your life whom you associate with the energy of ***the Snake***?

- Yes (describe how): ____________
- No

How do you relate to the idea of being strategic or clever in your daily life?

- It comes naturally to me.
- I struggle with planning.
- Other: ____________

If ***The Snake*** were a lesson for you, what do you think it would try to teach you?

- Adaptation
- Protection
- Reflection before acting.
- Other: ____________

How could you transform the energy of the Snake into something positive for yourself?

THE COFFIN

What feelings does ***the Coffin*** evoke when it appears in a spread?

- Sadness
- Transformation
- Fear
- Other: ___________

Do you recall a moment in your life when you had to let go of something or someone?

- Yes (briefly describe): ___________
- No

How do you perceive endings in your life?

- As opportunities for rebirth.
- As something difficult to accept.
- Other: ___________

If ***the Coffin*** symbolized a cycle you need to close, what would it be?

- Toxic relationships
- A negative habit
- Fears of change
- Other: ___________

What positive word could you associate with ***the Coffin*** after reflecting on its meaning?

THE SCYTHE

What is the first thing you think or feel when you see ***the Scythe***, in a spread?

- Fear
- Decision
- Finality
- Other: __________

Do you recall a moment in your life when you had to make a drastic decision?

- Yes (briefly describe): __________
- No

What does the act of "cutting" symbolize for you?

- Loss
- Liberation
- Change
- Other: __________

If you could use ***the Scythe*** as a tool to transform something in your life, what would it be?

- Relationships
- Habits
- Fears
- Other: __________

What positive word could you associate with the Scythe after reflecting on its meaning?

THE WHIP

What emotions arise in you when you see ***the Whip*** in a reading?

- Tension
- Energy
- Repetition
- Other: ____________

Are there repetitive patterns in your life that cause conflict or frustration?

- Yes (briefly describe them): ____________
- No

How do you handle conflicts or arguments in your environment?

- Avoiding them.
- Facing them.
- Other: ____________

If the Whip invited you to break a repetitive cycle, what would you do differently?

What positive action could you take today to transform the energy of the Whip into something constructive?

THE FOX

What immediately comes to mind when you see ***the Fox***, on a spread?

- Distrust
- Strategy
- Caution
- Other: ____________

Is there a situation in your life that requires more cleverness or care?

- Yes (describe it): ____________
- No

How do you relate to the idea of acting strategically in demanding situations?

- It comes naturally to me.
- I prefer to avoid it.
- Other: ____________

If ***the Fox*** could give you advice to improve your life, what do you think it would be?

What positive word could you associate with the Fox after reflecting on its meaning?

THE MOUNTAIN

What feeling do you get when you see ***the Mountain*** on a card spread?

- Blockage
- Challenge
- Persistence
- Other: ______________

What obstacle do you feel you are currently facing in your life?

- Personal
- Professional
- Emotional
- Other: ______________

How do you usually face significant challenges?

- With patience and determination.
- By avoiding or delaying them.
- Other: ______________

If the Mountain symbolized an opportunity for growth, what lesson do you think you could learn from it?

What positive image could you associate with the Mountain to see it as an achievable challenge?

THE MICE

What emotions does ***the Mice*** card evoke in you?

- Anxiety
- Loss
- Wear
- Other: ____________

Is there something in your life that you feel is draining your energy or resources?

- Yes (briefly describe it): ____________
- No

How do you usually manage small losses or wear in your life?

- Ignoring them.
- Addressing them immediately.
- Other: ____________

If ***the Mice*** were an opportunity to identify the unnecessary, what would you eliminate from your life?

What positive word could you associate with ***the Mice*** after reflecting on its meaning?

THE CROSS

What do you feel when you see ***the Cross*** in a reading?

- Burden
- Faith
- Resignation
- Other: ____________

What burden do you feel you are currently carrying in your life?

- Emotional
- Spiritual
- Physical
- Other: ____________

How do you manage responsibilities that seem heavy or unavoidable?

- With acceptance.
- By resisting or postponing.
- Other: ____________

If the Cross could help you find purpose in your burdens, what lesson do you think it would be showing you?

What positive symbol could you associate with the Cross to transform it into a sign of hope?

MEDITATION: RELEASING FEARS AND MISCONCEPTIONS

PURPOSE This exercise aims to help you release fears, emotional blocks, and misconceptions about Lenormand's negative cards. It also seeks to help you reconcile with their energies, seeing them as tools for learning and transformation.

PREPARATION

- Find a quiet place where you can relax without interruptions.
- Have your Lenormand deck handy and select the nine negative cards: Clouds, Snake, Coffin, Scythe, Whip, Fox, Mountain, Mice, and Cross.
- Arrange the cards in front of you, either in a circle or a straight line, depending on your preference.

STEP 1: INITIAL CONNECTION

1. Sit comfortably with your back straight and your hands relaxed on your knees.

Close your eyes and take three deep breaths:

- Inhale: Feel calm entering your body.
- Exhale: Let go of any tension or unease.

STEP 2: ENERGY VISUALIZATION

1. Visualize a golden ray of light descending toward you from the universe.

2. Imagine this light connecting your heart with each of the negative cards in front of you.

3. See how this light softens the energy of the cards, transforming any feelings of fear or rejection into acceptance and curiosity.

STEP 3: DIALOGUE WITH THE CARDS

1. Open your eyes and observe each card individually.

2. As you look at a card, ask yourself:

- "What message do you have for me?"
- "What do I need to learn from you?"

3. Pay close attention to any thoughts, images, or emotions that arise and write them down in a journal.

STEP 4: RELEASE MANTRA

1. With all the cards in front of you, place your hands over your heart and repeat the following mantra aloud or silently:

   "I accept the lessons these cards bring into my life. I release fear and open myself to learning and transformation."

2. Feel the energy of acceptance filling your body and mind.

STEP 5: CLOSURE AND GRATITUDE

1. Thank the cards for their messages and teachings.

2. Place the cards back into your deck with the intention of using them as tools of wisdom, not fear.

ADDITIONAL TIP

This exercise can be repeated whenever you resist the negative cards or need to deepen your understanding of their symbolism. You can complement this meditation with your reflective questionnaire, reviewing your responses after the exercise to notice any changes in your perspective.

"Myths shape our fears; understanding them reveals the hidden wisdom within the cards."

Note: Image created by Liz Figueroa with AI

Common Myths and Beliefs About the Negative Lenormand Cards

Throughout history, the negative cards of Lenormand have captivated readers with their air of mystery, profound symbolism, and deep connection to universal human experiences. From the commanding presence of the Scythe to the elusive enigma of the Clouds, these cards invite us to uncover not just their messages, but also the rich tapestry of beliefs and myths that surround them. They challenge us to delve deeper, forging a sense of understanding and connection that transcends the surface of a reading.

In this section, we'll explore the evolving interpretations of these cards, tracing their roots through cultural and spiritual concepts that have shaped their symbolism. Myths and beliefs are not mere stories—they are keys that unlock new dimensions of meaning, encouraging a more open-minded and enlightened perspective. By embracing these narratives, we gain insight into how biases and traditions shape our understanding of the cards, empowering us to see them with fresh clarity.

Each myth presented here is more than a tale—it's a doorway to a deeper understanding, where symbolism and practicality merge to enhance our connection with the Lenormand oracle. As you journey through these pages, you may not only unravel the mysteries of the negative cards but also discover tools for personal growth and self-reflection. Let these insights inspire and empower you to approach your readings—and your own path of development—with renewed confidence and purpose.

MYTH/BELIEF NO. 1:
THE SCYTHE CUTS OR HARVESTS

The Scythe is one of the most enigmatic cards in Lenormand due to its dual symbolism. This duality is significant as it allows the card to represent both destructive and constructive forces. Is it a destructive tool or an instrument of harvest? Traditionally, it is interpreted as a card of drastic cuts and abrupt decisions, evoking images of separation and danger. However, in the agricultural context, the Scythe symbolizes the harvest—a time of reaping the fruits of one's labor. This duality creates a paradox that confuses many students but enriches the card's meaning and implications in readings.

From a human perspective, the Scythe reflects sudden changes that, while painful, are necessary to make room for the new. For instance, ending a relationship may feel like a deep cut, but it can free someone from a connection that no longer serves them. This symbolism of destruction and creation is not just a concept in tarot, but it's deeply rooted in our everyday lives, making the audience feel connected and engaged.

The myth of the Scythe also invites readers to consider the context in which it appears. The Scythe can represent a positive harvest after significant effort when paired with cards like the Sun or the Clover. On the other hand, when combined with cards like the Mice or the Cross, its meaning tends to lean toward a painful cut. Understanding this card means embracing its ambiguous nature and potential to transform us. It's a challenge, but one that can be deeply motivating.

MYTH/BELIEF NO. 2:
THE SNAKE AND THE FOX, TWO FEMALES OF DANGER

The Snake and the Fox have historically been associated with the image of women as cunning, manipulative, or dangerous. This symbolism reflects cultural narratives where women who defied social norms were seen as threats. In Lenormand, these cards often represent females with hidden intentions or calculated strategies, perpetuating this archetype.

However, it is important to remember that these cards do not always signify danger. The Snake can symbolize transformation and adaptability, while the Fox speaks to intelligent survival in adverse circumstances. Both cards have the potential for positive interpretations, embodying qualities that can be helpful or harmful, depending on the context in which they appear. For instance, in a work-related reading, the Fox might represent ingenuity and creativity rather than deceit.

Exploring this myth is an opportunity for students to challenge their own biases. Why are cunning and strategy often seen as negative when linked to women? Understanding the Snake and the Fox from a balanced perspective is a crucial step for readers to overcome these preconceived ideas and appreciate these cards as symbols of strength and adaptability.

MYTH/BELIEF NO. 3:
THE COFFIN AND THE MICE, TWO PERSPECTIVES ON LOSS

The Coffin and the Mice share a common theme: loss. However, the way they represent this concept differs significantly. The Coffin symbolizes central and inevitable endings, while the Mice reflect more minor but persistent losses that wear down over time. This contrast raises a thought-provoking question: which is more challenging to face, a significant loss or a series of small absences?

From a symbolic perspective, the Coffin beckons us to accept the end of cycles, representing the transformation that follows a definitive ending. In contrast, the Mice symbolize the anxiety and daily wear caused by unresolved issues, demanding immediate action to halt their cumulative weight. These symbols, while different in their representation of loss, both underscore the need for proactive responses.

This myth underscores the need to address both types of losses with wisdom. The Coffin, with its call for acceptance and deep reflection, stands in contrast to the Mice, which demand immediate action to halt the erosion caused by unresolved issues. Together, these symbols serve as a powerful reminder that loss, while universal and often painful, can also be a catalyst for transformation when approached with the right mindset.

MYTH/BELIEF NO. 4:
THE WHIP AND THE CROSS AS PUNISHMENT AND REPENTANCE

The Whip and the Cross share an energy that evokes suffering and self-infliction, connecting them to cultural narratives of punishment and repentance. In many traditions, the Whip is seen as a symbol of physical discipline, often linked to the atonement of guilt. In some card decks, it is depicted with friars engaging in self-flagellation, reinforcing the idea of redemption through pain. On the other hand, the Cross is associated with the burden of fate and is often seen in cemeteries as a reminder of sacrifices and inevitable endings.

From a spiritual perspective, both cards confront us with the need to face our guilt and responsibilities. The Whip represents the repetitive cycle of self-reproach or internal conflicts that we must break, while the Cross invites us to accept trials as part of a greater purpose. Although the suffering they symbolize may seem inescapable, they also carry a lesson: pain can transform into strength if faced with faith and courage, underlining the importance of these virtues in spiritual growth.

This myth reflects how punishment and repentance are universal human experiences but not definitive ones. In a reading, these cards may indicate the need to release self-imposed burdens or find redemption through forgiveness. Paired with cards like the Sun or the Stars, they suggest that even in suffering, there is not just room, but a potential for hope and profound spiritual transformation, uplifting and encouraging us all.

MYTH/BELIEF NO. 5:
THE MOUNTAIN AS AN OBSTACLE AND DISTANCE

The Mountain is a card that often confuses students due to its ambiguity. Is it simply an obstacle to overcome, or does it also represent a distance that doesn't necessarily involve resistance? In Lenormand tradition, the Mountain embodies imposing barriers that block the way. Still, its symbolism also encompasses the idea of physical or emotional separation, like a distant landscape keeping us disconnected from something or someone.

As an obstacle, the Mountain reflects significant challenges that demand patience and perseverance. This could be a financial issue, a work conflict, or a strained relationship. However, it's important to remember that every obstacle is an opportunity for growth and change. On the other hand, as a symbol of distance, it may point to emotional disconnection, physical separation, or a goal that seems out of reach. In both cases, the Mountain invites us to reflect on our determination and adaptability, and to see these challenges as opportunities for personal growth and change.

The myth of the Mountain also reminds us that not all obstacles are harmful, and not all separations are permanent. In a reading, the meaning of the Mountain is not fixed, but largely depends on the reader's interpretation and the surrounding cards. For example, paired with the Clover, it might indicate a temporary obstacle, while the Cross could symbolize a prolonged spiritual trial. Understanding this myth and trusting your interpretation is key to interpreting its message with clarity and balance, empowering you as a reader.

"Every card reflects a story, revealing the depth of human nature and the strength within us to transform challenges into growth."

Note: Image created by Liz Figueroa with AI

Exploring Human Aspects in the Negative Lenormand Cards

Have you ever wondered how Lenormand cards can reveal not just events, but the intricate stories of the people in your life? Each card holds the potential to uncover more than just surface-level meanings, and the negative cards, with their profound symbolism, offer a unique opportunity to explore the physical, emotional, and spiritual dimensions of those they represent. These cards invite you to dive deeper, empowering your readings with a richer understanding of human nature.

In this section, we'll explore how each negative card intricately describes a man or a woman, painting a vivid picture of their appearance, emotional state, and spiritual energy. These insights go beyond mere symbols—they connect you to the human dynamics behind the cards, adding layers of meaning and depth to your interpretations.

So, get ready to uncover how these cards can shed light on the people in your readings, offering descriptions that delve into the complexities of character and behavior. With this knowledge, you'll elevate your readings to a new level of insight and precision, leaving a lasting impact on those you guide.

THE CLOUDS

"Appearances can be deceiving; what seems uncertain may. also be profound."

Man or Woman Associated with Clouds

1. Physical Appearance:
    - A face with features reflecting melancholy or indecision, such as slightly furrowed brows.
    - Pale or dull-toned skin, giving an impression of exhaustion or stress.
    - Casual clothing, often disheveled or in gray tones, symbolizing uncertainty.

2. Emotional Aspect:
    - An introspective personality with a tendency to overthink.
    - Emotions may be unstable, alternating between hope and discouragement.
    - Difficulty expressing their feelings, leading to confusion in those around them.

3. Spiritual Aspect:
    - Individuals in constant search of clarity, often caught in deep questions about their purpose.
    - Their energy may feel scattered, as if they are dealing with a spiritual fog.
    - Enormous potential to find enlightenment once they overcome their internal doubts.

THE SNAKE

"Not everything that dazzles are trustworthy; observe before trusting."

Man or Woman Associated with the Snake

1. Physical Appearance:
    - Attractive yet enigmatic features, such as piercing eyes or a calculated smile.
    - Smooth and well-cared-for skin, symbolizing attention to detail.
    - Elegant or seductive style, often in deep colors like dark green or black.

2. Emotional Aspect:
    - Strategic individuals, often reserved about their intentions.
    - Persuasive and skilled at manipulating situations to their advantage.
    - Emotionally calculating, prioritizing their own interests over others.

3. Spiritual Aspect:
    - Energy is focused on transformation and personal growth.
    - May have connections to the occult or spiritual practices that help them maintain control.
    - Important lessons in honesty and authenticity on their spiritual journey.

THE COFFIN

“Change is not the end; it is the rebirth into something deeper.”

Man or Woman Associated with the Coffin

1. Physical Appearance:
    - A posture that conveys tiredness or introspection, such as slightly hunched shoulders.
    - Pale skin or a somber appearance, often in dark tones.
    - Modest clothing, sometimes with an "outdated" or melancholic style.

2. Emotional Aspect:
    - Deeply reflective individuals, often carrying nostalgia or melancholy.
    - Tend to resist change, clinging to what they consider safe.
    - Great capacity for healing and transformation once they accept the closure of cycles.

3. Spiritual Aspect:
    - Strong karmic lessons pushing them toward detachment and acceptance.
    - Introspective energy guiding them toward a profound understanding of death and renewal.
    - Can become powerful spiritual guides if they overcome their fears of change.

THE SCYTHE

"The courage to cut away the unnecessary is the first step toward freedom."

Man or Woman Associated with the Scythe

1. Physical Appearance:
   - Defined features, such as a strong jawline or angular facial structure.
   - Intense gaze, conveying determination.
   - Practical or functional clothing, often in red, black, or metallic tones.

2. Emotional Aspect:
   - Decisive individuals who are unafraid to make quick or drastic decisions.
   - May come across as cold or calculating under pressure.
   - Tend to sever ties quickly if they feel something no longer serves them.

3. Spiritual Aspect:
   - Transformative energy focuses on action and change.
   - Can act as catalysts for necessary endings in the lives of others.
   - Learn to balance their decision-making abilities with compassion and patience.

THE WHIP

"The repetition of conflict may hold the key to breaking it."

Man or Woman Associated with the Whip

1. Physical Appearance:
   - Athletic build or firm posture reflecting energy and constant movement.
   - Facial expression conveying intensity or tension.
   - Fitted or sporty clothing, often in bold colors like red, orange, or black.

2. Emotional Aspect:
   - Enthusiastic individuals with a tendency toward irritability or conflict.
   - React quickly, sometimes impulsively.
   - Need to learn how to manage the repetition of emotional conflict patterns.

3. Spiritual Aspect:
   - Dynamic energy is focused on overcoming challenges through effort.
   - Tend to face the same struggles until they learn the necessary lesson.
   - Great potential to channel their intensity into practices like active meditation or spiritual sports.

THE FOX

"Intelligence is not just about knowing but adapting to the moment."

Man or Woman Associated with the Fox

1. Physical Appearance:
   - Sharp or delicate features, indicating observation and precision.
   - Agile and quiet movements, with a watchful demeanor.
   - Discreet or minimalist clothing, often in earthy or neutral tones.

2. Emotional Aspect:
   - Cautious individuals who rarely reveal their true intentions.
   - Strong survival instincts, often prioritizing themselves.
   - May come across as distrustful or calculating in relationships.

3. Spiritual Aspect:
   - Adaptive energy that allows them to learn from even the most challenging circumstances.
   - Tend to explore practical or self-focused spiritual paths.
   - Learn to balance their cleverness with honesty and authenticity.

THE MOUNTAIN

"Obstacles are opportunities to reach heights you never imagined."

Man or Woman Associated with the Mountain

1. Physical Appearance:
    - An imposing figure with a presence that conveys strength.
    - A serious or distant face, with expressions reflecting patience.
    - Durable or functional clothing, often in dark or earthy tones.

2. Emotional Aspect:
    - Persistent individuals with great capacity to endure difficulties.
    - May be perceived as reserved or distant due to their focus on challenges.
    - Tend to build strong but slow relationships.

3. Spiritual Aspect:
    - Resilient energy that connects them with patience and perseverance.
    - Often have a spiritual approach rooted through discipline and persistence.
    - Learn that obstacles are teachers that strengthen the soul.

THE MICE

"Even what seems small can drain the greatest if left unattended."

Man or Woman Associated with the Mice

1. Physical Appearance:
   - Slim build or slightly unkempt appearance.
   - Nervous or restless movements, with a gaze that denotes worry.
   - Practical but untidy clothing, often in muted or neutral tones.

2. Emotional Aspect:
   - Individuals, who tend to worry about small things, often letting accumulations affect them emotionally.
   - May feel easily drained due to their focus on problems.
   - Need to learn to let go of what they cannot control.

3. Spiritual Aspect:
   - Energy, that teaches the importance of eliminating the unnecessary to preserve the essential.
   - Tend to explore spiritual practices focused on cleansing or purification.
   - Learn to transform wear into renewal and strength.

THE CROSS

"The weight you carry is the path to your highest purpose."

Man or Woman Associated with the Cross

1. Physical Appearance:
    - Posture that conveys strength but also an emotional or physical burden.
    - Facial expressions reflecting seriousness and focus.
    - Simple and sober clothing, often in dark or symbolic colors like red or purple.

2. Emotional Aspect:
    - Individuals who carry significant responsibilities or life lessons.
    - Tend to sacrifice themselves for others, which can lead to emotional fatigue.
    - Find strength in their faith and inner resilience.

3. Spiritual Aspect:
    - Energy is deeply connected to karmic and spiritual purpose.
    - Tend to explore practices of faith or devotion to overcome their trials.
    - Learn that every burden is an opportunity to achieve enlightenment.

CONTRASTS BETWEEN NEGATIVE AND POSITIVE CARDS IN LENORMAND

Understanding how energies interact within a situation is a key aspect of Lenormand card interpretation. Classifying cards as negative, positive, or neutral sets the tone of the reading. While initially discouraging, negative cards take on different nuances when surrounded by positive or neutral cards. These combinations can soften their impact or even offer a more constructive interpretation.

Consider the transformative power of highly positive cards like the Sun, Bouquet, or Key. These cards can effectively alter the tone of a reading, turning a negative message into something more hopeful. They often indicate a favorable resolution or significant learning after a challenge.

Neutral cards like the Letter and the Book play a crucial role in softening the impact of a negative card like the Fox. They can lead the reading to a more neutral point, suggesting that strategic communication or research requires caution and careful analysis. In this context, the Fox is not necessarily deceitful but a suggestion to act intelligently and cautiously in handling information.

HOW THE POSITIVE CARDS INFLUENCE NEGATIVE ONES

1. **SOFTENING THE IMPACT**:
Positive cards reduce the severity of negative cards, offering a more optimistic perspective.

Example:
Cross + *Sun*: The Cross indicates sacrifices and emotional burdens, but the Sun softens this weight by promising success and relief after effort.

2. **NEUTRALIZATION:**
In some combinations, positive and negative cards can balance each other, creating a neutral or less extreme message.

Example:
Mountain + *Clover*: While the Mountain represents a significant obstacle, the Clover indicates it will be temporary and manageable.

3. **TRANSFORMATION:**
Positive cards can completely change the context of a negative card, showing how difficulties can turn into opportunities.

Example:
Mice + *Sun*: The Mice signal losses or wear, but the Sun assures a bright and optimistic recovery.

EXAMPLES OF CONTRASTS WITH NEGATIVE AND POSITIVE CARDS

THE CLOUDS

Example: *Clouds + Star + Bouquet*

The Clouds show confusion or uncertainty, but the Star indicates hope, and the Bouquet assures a harmonious resolution.

THE SNAKE

Example: Snake + Key + Heart

The Snake signals obstacles or deceit, but the Key indicates solutions, and the Heart shows that sincerity will prevail.

THE COFFIN

Example: Coffin + Sun + Ship

The Coffin marks an ending, but the Sun assures success after that closure, and the Ship indicates continuous progress toward new goals.

THE SCYTHE

Example: Scythe + Bouquet + Tower

The Scythe suggests an abrupt cut, but the Bouquet softens this change with harmony, and the Tower assures stability after the transition.

THE WHIP

Example: Whip + Bouquet + Anchor

The Whip suggests conflicts, but the Bouquet shows reconciliation, and the Anchor ensures long-term stability.

THE FOX

Example: Fox + Clover + Moon

The Fox highlights necessary cunning, but the Clover promises quick success, and the Moon ensures positive recognition after the effort.

THE MOUNTAIN

Example: Mountain + Key + Sun

The Mountain indicates significant obstacles, but the Key and Sun together ensure they will be successfully overcome.

THE MICE

Example: Mice + Path + House

The Mice represent wear or loss, but the Path suggests a new direction, and the House ensures future stability.

THE CROSS

Example: Cross + Sun + Child

The Cross shows necessary sacrifices, but the Sun and the Child indicate a hopeful and joyful new beginning.

STRATEGIES FOR INTERPRETING CONTRASTS

1. ***Manage Your Emotions***:
   - Do not assume a negative card is entirely bad or that a positive card will fix everything. Look at the combination as a whole.

2. ***Consider Polarities:***
   - Observe how positive cards soften or intensify the impact of negative cards.

3. ***Use the Context of the Question:***
   - Adjust the interpretation based on the query. The same combination can mean different things depending on the topic (love, work, health, etc.).

4. ***Perspective Approach:***
   - View the reading from an overarching perspective. Ask yourself: What overall balance does this combination reveal?

NEGATIVE LENORMAND CARDS AS BRIDGES OF ENERGY

Negative Lenormand cards are commonly interpreted as warning signs, challenges, or blockages. However, observing their interaction with the surrounding cards, we discover that many of them function as 'bridges' connecting opposing energies in a reading. These cards not only reflect difficulties but also show the transition from an adverse situation to a positive resolution or change. The key to understanding their true meaning lies in the context of the spread, which can provide crucial insights into the querent's situation and the potential for growth or change.

The concept of negative cards as 'bridges' allows readers to see how energy flows within a spread. For instance, cards like the Clouds, with their dual visual polarities, can act as a transition between an obstacle represented by the Mountain and a favorable outcome symbolized by the Bouquet. Similarly, the Whip can bridge the gap between conflict (represented by the Snake) and resolution (symbolized by the Sun). By understanding this movement of energy, readers can interpret the dynamics of change in the querent's life more accurately.

Recognizing negative cards as mediators reduces the emotional impact they often generate and provides a broader and more hopeful perspective in readings. This approach shifts the narrative from "problems" to "processes," helping Lenormand readers guide their queries with clarity and confidence, even in the most complex spreads.

.

EXPLAINING THE CONCEPT: NEGATIVE CARDS AS BRIDGES OF ENERGY

The Role of Negative Cards as Connectors:

Negative cards do not always represent permanent endings or blockages. In fewer spreads, they function as transitions between opposing energies, revealing the natural flow of events. For example, the Scythe may signify an abrupt cut that leads to an unexpected solution.

How to Identify a "Bridge" Card:

- A negative card appearing between two positive cards can act as a mediator.
- If the negative card is surrounded by neutral cards, its influence will be moderate.
- If it is next to other negative cards, it may intensify the challenge but can still signal the beginning of a change.

Reading Energy Flow:

Observe how the cards before and after the negative card influence its message. For instance:

- Before: What energy leads to the negative card?
- After: What energy follows after facing that challenge?

THE CLOUDS

Acts as a transition from confusion to clarity.

Example: ***Mountain*** *+* ***Clouds*** *+* ***Bouquet***

The Mountain indicates an obstacle, while the Clouds show a period of uncertainty. However, the Bouquet ensures the situation will culminate positively.

THE SNAKE

Highlights complications or detours that eventually lead to a resolution.

Example: ***Stork*** *+* ***Snake*** *+* ***Ring***

The Snake shows obstacles in a change, but the Ring ensures that commitment or the goal will be achieved.

THE COFFIN

Marks the end of a cycle to make way for a new one.

Example: ***Ship*** *+* ***Coffin*** *+* ***Sun***

The Coffin shows the end of an emotional journey, but the Sun promises clarity and success after that closure.

THE SCYTHE

Marks an abrupt cut that transforms a stagnant situation.

Example: ***Mice + Scythe + Sun***

The Mice indicate wear; the Scythe cuts it at the root, and the Sun shows that this will lead to clarity and success.

THE WHIP

Represents tensions or conflicts that lead to a resolution.

Example: ***Heart + Whip + Tower***

The Whip suggests emotional conflicts, but the Tower ensures that this will strengthen the structure of the relationship.

THE FOX

Indicates necessary strategies to manage a tricky situation.

Example: ***Moon + Fox + Bouquet***

The Fox suggests caution, but the Bouquet ensures that the strategy will result in positive outcomes.

THE MOUNTAIN

Indicates a significant obstacle that can be overcome with patience.

Example: ***Clover*** + ***Mountain*** + ***Key***

Although the Mountain hinders progress, the Key ensures that a solution is within reach.

THE MICE

Acts as gradual wear that leads to the need for change.

Example: ***Fish*** + ***Mice*** + ***Path***

The Mice show financial losses, but the Path indicates that a new direction will resolve the issue.

THE CROSS

Represents necessary sacrifices to achieve a spiritual or practical outcome.

Example: ***Star*** + ***Cross*** + ***Key***

The Star shows hope; the Cross indicates a sacrifice, but the Key ensures that this sacrifice will open new opportunities.

"Every interpretation is a doorway, where understanding the common unlocks the extraordinary."

Note: Image created by Liz Figueroa with AI

Common Interpretations of the Negative Lenormand Cards

Lenormand's negative cards' standard and traditional meanings represent the most widely accepted interpretations. These definitions, passed down through the years, provide a solid foundation for understanding the symbolism of each card. Importantly, they also reflect cultural perceptions and human experiences, which play a significant role in shaping their interpretation. This cultural awareness is key to a nuanced understanding of the cards.

This section is designed to give you a clear and concise idea of how these cards are perceived in their most basic contexts. However, as a reader, it is always important to remember that each card can take on different nuances depending on the question, the combinations, and the adjacent cards. For instance, the Snake card can represent deceit in a question about relationships, but it can also signify wisdom when paired with the Book card.

Exploring these traditional meanings is crucial for any tarot reader. It will help you better understand the negative cards, giving you the confidence to integrate them into your readings with greater clarity and perspective. Understanding these meanings is like learning the grammar of a language-it provides the structure and rules that allow you to form coherent and meaningful sentences, or in this case, readings.

THE CLOUDS

"The storm always gives way to the sun,
if you wait long enough."

Traditional Meaning

Confusion, doubts, temporary worries, states of uncertainty. Can represent a situation lacking clarity or vision.

Element

Air: Represents changeability, intangibility, and what is difficult to grasp.

Polarity

Negative: Creates unease and ambiguity in readings.

Movement

Slow and variable: Can change direction depending on the surrounding cards.

Astrological Attributes

Gemini or Mercury: Associated with duality, confusing communication, and scattered thoughts.

Numerological Aspect

Number 6: Symbolizes duality, the search for balance, and internal challenges.

Example Spreads

Clouds + Sun + Anchor: A period of confusion at work will clear up and lead to lasting stability.
Clouds + Heart + Lily: Temporary doubts in a romantic relationship that can be resolved with patience and honesty.

THE SNAKE

"Every curve in the path brings a hidden lesson."

Traditional Meaning
Deception, manipulation, setbacks, or unexpected detours. Can represent a cunning person or a situation that is not as it seems.

Element
Water: Represents hidden emotions, cunning, and the winding flow of life.

Polarity
Negative: Generates distrust and alertness in readings.

Movement
Curved and winding: Proceeds strategically and unpredictably.

Astrological Attributes
Scorpio or Pluto: Associated with transformation, the occult, and secrets.

Numerological Aspect
Number 7: Symbolizes deep analysis, introspection, and emotional challenges.

Example Spreads
Snake + *Clouds* + *Mice*: A deceptive situation creates confusion and material or emotional losses.
Snake + *Ring* + *Clover*: A relationship with hidden tensions that, with luck, can be resolved.

THE COFFIN

"Endings are the beginning of something greater."

Traditional Meaning
Endings, closures, profound transformation, and inevitable changes. Can indicate mourning, loss, or the need to let go of something.

Element
Earth: Represents the cycle of life and the connection to the material world.

Polarity
Negative: Evokes a sense of finality or limitation.

Movement
Static: Represents a state of pause or definitive termination.

Astrological Attributes
Capricorn or Saturn: Associated with structures, karma, and tough lessons.

Numerological Aspect
Number 8: Symbolizes transformation, power, and regeneration.

Example Spreads
Coffin + Tree + Sun: A cycle of illness ends, leading to recovery.
Coffin + Child + Lily: The closure of a childhood phase gives way to a more mature emotional peace.

THE SCYTHE

"A drastic cut frees what no longer serves."

Traditional Meaning
Quick cuts, drastic decisions, necessary separations. Can indicate danger or something happening suddenly.

Element
Fire: Represents swift action, determination, and power.

Polarity
Neutral-Negative: Can be negative or liberating depending on the context.

Movement
Rapid: Acts with force and without prior notice.

Astrological Attributes
Mars or Aries: Associated with action, strength, and courage.

Numerological Aspect
Number 10: Symbolizes important decisions and significant changes.

Example Spreads
Scythe + *Sun* + *Lily*: A drastic decision brings harmony and clarity.
Scythe + *Cross* + *Anchor*: A painful sacrifice results in future stability.

THE WHIP

"In repetition, we find both conflict and solution."

Traditional Meaning
Arguments, conflicts, recurring tensions, or repetitive strains. Can represent unhealthy habits or a conflicting routine.

Element
Fire: Represents intense energy, aggression, and repetitive motion.

Polarity
Negative: Creates friction and wear in readings.

Movement
Repetitive and fast: Reflects ongoing cycles that are not easily broken.

Astrological Attributes
Sagittarius or Mars: Associated with confrontation, repetitive effort, and intensity.

Numerological Aspect
Number 11: Symbolizes the duality of conflict and the opportunity for resolution.

Example Spreads
Whip + Mice + Cross: Repeated conflicts causing physical and emotional wear.
Whip + Anchor + Sun: An intense routine that, with effort, will lead to positive results.

THE FOX

"Cunning is a tool, not a weapon."

Traditional Meaning
Cunning, deception, survival, and hidden strategies. Can indicate a warning about unreliable people or situations.

Element
Earth: Represents practicality, mundaneness, and the need to adapt.

Polarity
Neutral-Negative: Can be a useful tool or a trap depending on the context.

Movement
Stealthy: Acts in the shadows, progressing undetected.

Astrological Attributes
Virgo or Mercury: Associated with analysis, intelligence, and adaptability.

Numerological Aspect
Number 14: Symbolizes the need to carefully evaluate before acting.

Example Spreads
Fox + Mice + Ring: An association that seems promising but hides deception.
Fox + Tree + Child: Intelligent adaptation to overcome challenges related to health or new beginnings.

THE MOUNTAIN

"Every obstacle is an opportunity in disguise."

Traditional Meaning
Obstacles, blockages, resistance, and slowness. Can indicate challenges that require patience and perseverance.

Element
Earth: Represents solidity, permanence, and stability.

Polarity
Negative: Creates stagnation and frustration in readings.

Movement
Static: Represents obstacles that are difficult to move or overcome.

Astrological Attributes
Capricorn or Saturn: Associated with prolonged effort, discipline, and tough lessons.

Numerological Aspect
Number 21: Symbolizes resilience, constant effort, and delayed rewards.

Example Spreads
Mountain + Sun + Clover: An obstacle that is overcome with optimism and a stroke of luck.
Mountain + Heart + Cross: Emotional challenges that require strength and faith.

THE MICE

"The small things we ignore can wear us down in big ways."

Traditional Meaning
Losses, deterioration, wear, and theft. Can represent something that slowly consumes energy or resources.

Element
Earth: Represents what deteriorates or disappears over time.

Polarity
Negative: Creates wear and constant worry.

Movement
Rapid but destructive: Acts silently yet with impact.

Astrological Attributes
Cancer or Saturn: Associated with emotions tied to loss and limitation.

Numerological Aspect
Number 23: Symbolizes energetic wear and the need to eliminate the unnecessary.

Example Spreads
Mice + Sun + Stars: A loss that leads to renewed clarity and hope.
Mice + House + Scythe: Significant material losses at home due to an abrupt decision.

THE CROSS

"The burden you carry now is the faith that will
take you farther."

Traditional Meaning
Suffering, burden, faith, and destiny. Can represent necessary sacrifices or karmic lessons.

Element
Fire: Represents the intensity of the trial and spiritual strength.

Polarity
Neutral-Negative: Can be challenging but also profoundly meaningful.

Movement
Heavy and static: Acts as a fixed point that cannot be avoided.

Astrological Attributes
Sagittarius or Saturn: Associated with destiny, spirituality, and tests of faith.

Numerological Aspect
Number 36: Symbolizes final challenges and significant achievements through sacrifice.

Example Spreads
Cross + Stars + Sun: A difficult sacrifice that ultimately brings clarity and success.
Cross + Anchor + Child: Heavy responsibilities limiting new beginnings but necessary for stability.

EXPLORING COMBINATIONS OF NEGATIVE LENORMAND CARDS

The negative cards of Lenormand, with their profound symbolism and powerful messages, are often seen as a challenge by readers. However, fully understanding them is key to unlocking their potential in any reading. This section is a comprehensive and practical resource to help you interpret these cards in various contexts.

In the first part, you will find details about each negative card: its traditional meaning, symbolic attributes, and how it reflects human experiences. In the second part, we present a glossary of combinations, where each negative card interacts with the 35 remaining cards in the deck, offering clear and contextual interpretations.

This glossary is more than a guide; it is a tool to deepen your practice and build confidence when working with negative cards. Here, you will find inspiration, clarity, and a solid foundation to make the most of the symbolism of these cards in your readings.

THE CLOUDS:

- Clouds + Rider: Confusing news or uncertain changes.
- Clouds + Clover: A brief phase of doubts with a positive resolution.
- Clouds + Ship: Confusion or uncertainty related to travel or movement.
- Clouds + House: Doubts or concerns about home or family.
- Clouds + Tree: Concerns related to health or well-being.
- Clouds + Snake: Manipulation or deception causing confusion.
- Clouds + Coffin: Financial insecurity or concern about investments.
- Clouds + Flowers: Doubts about an offer or social event.
- Clouds + Scythe: A drastic decision that clears doubts or generates uncertainty.
- Clouds + Whip: Verbal conflicts or persistent tensions.
- Clouds + Bird: Conversations or news that are unclear.
- Clouds + Child: Insecurity in a new beginning or stage.
- Clouds + Fox: Deception that clouds the perception of the truth.
- Clouds + Bear: Concerns related to finances or authority.
- Clouds + Star: Lack of clarity in goals or aspirations.
- Clouds + Stork: Changes that generate initial uncertainty.

- Clouds + Dog: Doubts about a friend's loyalty or trustworthiness.
- Clouds + Tower: Confusion related to institutions or legal decisions.
- Clouds + Garden: Uncertainty in social events or community circles.
- Clouds + Mountain: Mental or emotional obstacle that generates confusion.
- Clouds + Path: Indecision in an important choice.
- Clouds + Rats: Concerns that lead to small losses or wear.
- Clouds + Heart: Doubts in a romantic relationship.
- Clouds + Ring: Confusion about a commitment or contract.
- Clouds + Book: Hidden information that creates uncertainty.
- Clouds + Letter: Ambiguous or misinterpreted message.
- Clouds + Man: A man facing doubts or uncertainty.
- Clouds + Woman: A woman dealing with confusion or concerns.
- Clouds + Lily: Confusion in matters of peace, harmony, or family relationships.
- Clouds + Sun: Clarity comes after a period of doubt.
- Clouds + Moon: Emotional insecurity or creative uncertainty.
- Clouds + Key: Lack of clarity in a solution or answer.
- Clouds + Fish: Confusion related to financial flows.
- Clouds + Anchor: Static depression or lack of progress.
- Clouds + Cross: Emotional or spiritual suffering caused by doubts.

THE SNAKE:

- Snake + Rider: A clever message or news related to deception.
- Snake + Clover: A quick resolution to a complicated problem.
- Snake + Ship: A journey filled with detours or possible complications.
- Snake + House: Manipulation or distrust within the family environment.
- Snake + Tree: Health problems related to stress or hidden situations.
- Snake + Clouds: Confusion caused by deception or manipulation.
- Snake + Coffin: Gains obtained in a questionable manner.
- Snake + Flowers: Flattery with hidden or dishonest intentions.
- Snake + Scythe: Sudden end to a manipulative situation.
- Snake + Whip: Conflicts generated by a clever or manipulative person.
- Snake + Bird: Tense conversations or rumors generated by intrigue.
- Snake + Child: Caution needed in new beginnings or situations.
- Snake + Fox: Cunning and deception working together.
- Snake + Bear: Manipulation or strategies related to power or finances.
- Snake + Star: Desires or goals achieved through unclear strategies.

- Snake + Stork: Changes involving detours or complications.
- Snake + Dog: A friend who cannot be fully trusted.
- Snake + Tower: Intrigues or manipulations in an institution or hierarchical environment.
- Snake + Garden: Hidden strategies in social events or public circles.
- Snake + Mountain: An obstacle generated by distrust or manipulations.
- Snake + Path: An unexpected detour that requires caution.
- Snake + Rats: Losses caused by manipulation or deception.
- Snake + Heart: Complicated relationships with possible betrayals or distrust.
- Snake + Ring: A commitment with hidden or dishonest intentions.
- Snake + Book: Secrets revealing manipulations or deception.
- Snake + Letter: A message with hidden or unclear intentions.
- Snake + Man: A man with a cunning or manipulative energy.
- Snake + Woman: A strategic, seductive, or manipulative woman.
- Snake + Lily: Complications related to peace, harmony, or sexual issues.
- Snake + Sun: Clarity about a complicated situation.
- Snake + Moon: Manipulative emotions or creativity used strategically.
- Snake + Key: Strategic solution to a complex problem.
- Snake + Fish: Strategies or manipulations related to finances.

- Snake + Anchor: Long-term manipulation.
- Snake + Cross: Strategies or manipulations that generate suffering.

THE COFFIN:

- Coffin + Rider: News about an important end or transformation.
- Coffin + Clover: A brief closure that brings new opportunities.
- Coffin + Ship: End of a journey or transformation related to movement.
- Coffin + House: Deep changes related to home or family.
- Coffin + Tree: Ending a health or well-being stage, such as the end of an illness.
- Coffin + Clouds: A confusing end or uncertainty about a closure.
- Coffin + Snake: End of manipulation or hidden strategy.
- Coffin + Flowers: A joyful stage coming to an end.
- Coffin + Scythe: Abrupt and inevitable transformation.
- Coffin + Whip: Conflicts that end or repetitive cycles that close.
- Coffin + Bird: Conversations about an end or loss.
- Coffin + Child: Ending a new beginning or a closure affecting something new.
- Coffin + Fox: End of a deceptive or strategic situation.
- Coffin + Bear: Deep transformation in matters of power or finances.

- Coffin + Star: Goals or dreams reaching a closure to open new possibilities.
- Coffin + Stork: A transformative change following a closure.
- Coffin + Dog: End of a friendship or loyal relationship.
- Coffin + Tower: Closure related to institutions or hierarchical structures.
- Coffin + Garden: Ending a connection with social circles or public events.
- Coffin + Mountain: A persistent obstacle coming to an end.
- Coffin + Path: Closing a chapter to choose a new direction.
- Coffin + Rats: A significant loss marking a closure.
- Coffin + Heart: End of an emotional or romantic relationship.
- Coffin + Ring: Breakup of a commitment or contract.
- Coffin + Book: End related to secrets or hidden information.
- Coffin + Letter: Message about a loss or significant closure.
- Coffin + Man: A man faces an important change or closure.
- Coffin + Woman: A woman goes through a significant transformation.
- Coffin + Lily: End of a stage leading to peace or renewal.
- Coffin + Sun: An end that brings clarity and success.
- Coffin + Moon: Emotions related to an end or spiritual transformation.
- Coffin + Key: Definitive solution or successful closure of a problem.

- Coffin + Fish: Transformation in financial or resource matters.
- Coffin + Anchor: Rest for a long time.
- Coffin + Cross: A karmic end or one related to sacrifices and faith.

THE SCYTHE:

- Scythe + Rider: Sudden news that requires quick decisions.
- Scythe + Clover: A drastic cut that brings a positive opportunity.
- Scythe + Ship: Abrupt changes related to travel or movement.
- Scythe + House: Transformation or significant decisions related to home.
- Scythe + Tree: Drastic interventions in health or well-being matters.
- Scythe + Clouds: Difficult decisions made amidst uncertainty.
- Scythe + Snake: Cutting ties with manipulations or deceptions.
- Scythe + Coffin: A drastic closure or abrupt transformation.
- Scythe + Flowers: An end affecting social relationships or events.
- Scythe + Whip: Conflicts that end suddenly.
- Scythe + Bird: Conversations leading to radical decisions.
- Scythe + Child: End of a stage or a drastic change in something new.
- Scythe + Fox: Cutting dishonest strategies or calculated deceptions.

- Scythe + Bear: Significant decisions related to power or finances.
- Scythe + Star: Drastic changes in personal goals or dreams.
- Scythe + Stork: Abrupt transformations in the family or environment.
- Scythe + Dog: Abrupt end of a friendship or loyal relationship.
- Scythe + Tower: Drastic decisions related to institutions or hierarchical structures.
- Scythe + Garden: Changes in social circles or community events.
- Scythe + Mountain: Sudden overcoming of a significant obstacle.
- Scythe + Path: A sudden decision at an important crossroads.
- Scythe + Rats: Cutting losses or eliminating significant wear and tear.
- Scythe + Heart: Abrupt end of an emotional relationship.
- Scythe + Ring: Breakup of a commitment or significant contract.
- Scythe + Book: Revelation of secrets that generates drastic changes.
- Scythe + Letter: A message that prompts important decisions.
- Scythe + Man: A man making radical decisions.
- Scythe + Woman: A woman facing significant transformations.
- Scythe + Lily: Changes leading to personal peace or harmony.
- Scythe + Sun: A cut that generates clarity or sudden success.

- Scythe + Moon: Deep emotional changes or creative transformations.
- Scythe + Key: A decision that opens new opportunities.
- Scythe + Fish: Drastic changes related to finances or resources.
- Scythe + Anchor: A drastic cut of security.
- Scythe + Cross: A necessary sacrifice to generate transformation.

THE WHIP:

- Whip + Rider: News that generates conflict or discussion.
- Whip + Clover: Minor conflicts or passing disagreements.
- Whip + Ship: Tension or disagreements related to a trip or relocation.
- Whip + House: Internal conflicts in the home or family disputes.
- Whip + Tree: Physical tension or conflicts related to health.
- Whip + Clouds: Confusing discussions or misinterpreted tensions.
- Whip + Snake: Conflicts related to manipulation or deception.
- Whip + Coffin: End of discussions or repetitive cycles.
- Whip + Flowers: Flattery with double intentions or tensions disguised as courtesy.
- Whip + Scythe: Conflicts that end abruptly or quick decisions following tension.

- Whip + Bird: Repetitive conversations or persistent disagreements.
- Whip + Child: Conflicts related to children or new beginnings.
- Whip + Fox: Tension caused by strategies or cunning.
- Whip + Bear: Power conflicts or financial tensions.
- Whip + Star: Discussion or tension in goals or aspirations.
- Whip + Stork: Changes that generate discussions or tense adjustments.
- Whip + Dog: Conflicts in friendships or loyalty relationships.
- Whip + Tower: Discussion or disagreements related to institutions or hierarchies.
- Whip + Garden: Conflicts in social or public environments.
- Whip + Mountain: Obstacles or prolonged tensions that generate conflict.
- Whip + Path: Difficulties in making decisions due to disagreements.
- Whip + Rats: Discussions that generate emotional or material wear.
- Whip + Heart: Emotional conflicts or tension in love relationships.
- Whip + Ring: Disputes within a commitment or contract.
- Whip + Book: Conflicts related to secrets or hidden information.
- Whip + Letter: A message that generates tension or misunderstandings.
- Whip + Man: A man facing tensions or repetitive conflicts.

- Whip + Woman: A woman dealing with constant discussions or tensions.
- Whip + Lily: Conflicts in search of peace or tensions related to harmony.
- Whip + Sun: Successful resolution of tensions or conflicts.
- Whip + Moon: Emotional tension or conflicts related to creativity.
- Whip + Key: A conflict that leads to a solution or unlocking.
- Whip + Fish: Disputes related to finances or resources.
- Whip + Anchor: An argument without a conclusion.
- Whip + Cross: Karmic conflicts or tensions that generate spiritual suffering.

THE FOX:

- Fox + Rider: News that requires caution or has hidden intentions.
- Fox + Clover: A clever solution that brings luck or quick results.
- Fox + Ship: A journey that requires care or hidden strategies.
- Fox + House: Caution in the family environment; possible deceptions at home.
- Fox + Tree: Cunning needed to face health challenges.
- Fox + Clouds: Confusion generated by strategies or deceptions.
- Fox + Snake: Intensified strategy; possible complex manipulation.

- Fox + Coffin: End of a deceptive or dishonest situation.
- Fox + Flowers: Flattery with hidden or strategic intentions.
- Fox + Scythe: Drastic decision to eliminate deceptions or manipulations.
- Fox + Whip: Conflicts caused by strategies or dishonesty.
- Fox + Bird: Conversations where caution is needed, or intentions should be analyzed.
- Fox + Child: Caution needed in a new beginning or project.
- Fox + Fox: Double strategy or extremely calculated situations.
- Fox + Bear: Strategy applied to power or financial matters.
- Fox + Star: Cunning applied to achieve goals or dreams.
- Fox + Stork: Changes that require adaptability or strategic caution.
- Fox + Dog: Caution in friendships or trust relationships.
- Fox + Tower: Strategies related to institutions or hierarchical decisions.
- Fox + Garden: Caution in social events or community circles.
- Fox + Mountain: An obstacle that can be overcome with strategy.
- Fox + Path: A choice that requires careful analysis or cunning.
- Fox + Rats: Losses caused by deceptions or hidden strategies.
- Fox + Heart: Relationships where trust may be compromised.

- Fox + Ring: A commitment that may involve dishonesty or hidden intentions.
- Fox + Book: Secrets that need to be handled with care or strategy.
- Fox + Letter: A message that requires analysis to detect hidden intentions.
- Fox + Man: A cunning, strategic man, or possibly dishonest.
- Fox + Woman: A cautious, strategic woman, or with hidden intentions.
- Fox + Lily: Strategies related to peace or personal balance.
- Fox + Sun: A strategy that leads to success or clarity.
- Fox + Moon: Emotional caution or creativity used strategically.
- Fox + Key: A solution that requires a strategic approach or caution.
- Fox + Fish: Strategies related to finances or economic flows.
- Fox + Anchor: Safe strategies.
- Fox + Cross: Strategies that generate emotional or karmic burdens.

THE MOUNTAIN:

- Mountain + Rider: News or progress blocked by an obstacle.
- Mountain + Clover: A temporary obstacle that can be overcome quickly.
- Mountain + Ship: Delays or blockages in a journey or movement.
- Mountain + House: An obstacle related to home or family.

- Mountain + Tree: A barrier or difficulty in health or well-being matters.
- Mountain + Clouds: An obstacle accompanied by confusion or lack of clarity.
- Mountain + Snake: A challenge caused by deception or manipulation.
- Mountain + Coffin: End of a persistent obstacle or change after a barrier.
- Mountain + Flowers: A social obstacle or one at celebratory events.
- Mountain + Scythe: An obstacle removed suddenly.
- Mountain + Whip: Prolonged conflicts or tension due to a blockage.
- Mountain + Bird: Tense conversations or concerns related to a blockage.
- Mountain + Child: A new beginning with initial obstacles.
- Mountain + Fox: An obstacle that requires cunning or strategy to overcome.
- Mountain + Bear: Blockage in matters of power or finances.
- Mountain + Star: An obstacle on the path to goals or aspirations.
- Mountain + Stork: Blocked changes or changes that are difficult to implement.
- Mountain + Dog: An obstacle related to friendships or loyalty.
- Mountain + Tower: Blockage related to institutions or bureaucracy.
- Mountain + Garden: Difficulties in a social or community environment.
- Mountain + Mountain: Intensified obstacle or persistent difficulty.

- Mountain + Path: Difficulty choosing a direction or overcoming an important crossroads.
- Mountain + Rats: Blockage that generates wear or gradual losses.
- Mountain + Heart: Emotional barrier or difficulty in romantic relationships.
- Mountain + Ring: A blocked commitment or a contract with difficulties.
- Mountain + Book: Hidden information that generates obstacles.
- Mountain + Letter: A message related to a blockage or persistent problem.
- Mountain + Man: A man facing a significant challenge.
- Mountain + Woman: A woman dealing with an emotional or practical barrier.
- Mountain + Lily: Obstacles that affect peace or personal harmony.
- Mountain + Sun: Successful overcoming of an obstacle.
- Mountain + Moon: Emotional obstacle or blockages in creativity.
- Mountain + Key: A solution that arises after overcoming a challenge.
- Mountain + Fish: Blockages in financial or economic flows.
- Mountain + Anchor: Long-lasting obstacles.
- Mountain + Cross: A karmic obstacle or spiritual burden that is hard to overcome.

THE RATS/MICE:

- Rats + Rider: News about losses or deterioration.
- Rats + Clover: A minor loss or one that is easily overcome.
-
- Rats + Ship: Financial wear or losses related to travel.
- Rats + House: Deterioration or problems in the family or home environment.
- Rats + Tree: Loss of energy or deterioration in health.
- Rats + Clouds: Losses caused by confusion or lack of clarity.
- Rats + Snake: Manipulations that generate losses or wear.
- Rats + Coffin: A significant loss marking the end of a stage.
- Rats + Flowers: Deterioration in social relationships or pleasant events.
- Rats + Scythe: Sudden or drastic loss.
- Rats + Whip: Wear caused by constant conflicts or arguments.
- Rats + Bird: Conversations about worries or minor losses.
- Rats + Child: Losses related to a new beginning or project.
- Rats + Fox: Losses due to dishonest strategies or deceptions.
- Rats + Bear: Wear or loss in matters of power or finances.
- Rats + Star: Difficulty achieving goals due to small obstacles.
- Rats + Stork: Changes that generate wear or gradual loss.

- Rats + Dog: Loss or deterioration in a friendship or trust relationship.
- Rats + Tower: Deterioration related to institutions or hierarchical structures.
- Rats + Garden: Wear in social or community environments.
- Rats + Mountain: Persistent losses caused by prolonged obstacles.
- Rats + Path: Decisions resulting in small inconveniences or losses.
- Rats + Heart: Emotional deterioration or wear in romantic relationships.
- Rats + Ring: Loss or wear in a commitment or contract.
- Rats + Book: Losses related to secrets or hidden information.
- Rats + Letter: A message related to worries or minor losses.
- Rats + Man: A man facing personal wear or loss.
- Rats + Woman: A woman dealing with minor losses or emotional wear.
- Rats + Lily: Wear in peace or personal harmony.
- Rats + Sun: Overcoming losses with clarity and eventual success.
- Rats + Moon: Emotional deterioration or creative wear.
- Rats + Key: A solution to stop the wear or loss.
- Rats + Fish: Economic losses or wear in financial flows.
- Rats + Anchor: Irreversible losses.
- Rats + Cross: Spiritual wear or prolonged suffering.

THE CROSS:

- Cross + Rider: News related to a burden or important lesson.
- Cross + Clover: A sacrifice that leads to a temporary or minor reward.
- Cross + Ship: A journey involving sacrifices or karmic trials.
- Cross + House: A burden or suffering related to home or family.
- Cross + Tree: Trials related to health or well-being.
- Cross + Clouds: Emotional or spiritual suffering due to confusion.
- Cross + Snake: A karmic lesson tied to manipulation or dishonesty.
- Cross + Coffin: A painful ending with a strong spiritual component.
- Cross + Flowers: Joy or celebration accompanied by a sacrifice.
- Cross + Scythe: A sudden sacrifice that generates emotional impact.
- Cross + Whip: Prolonged suffering due to conflicts or tensions.
- Cross + Bird: Conversations related to emotional burdens.
- Cross + Child: Sacrifice or trials related to a new beginning.
- Cross + Fox: Spiritual lessons linked to cunning or strategies.
- Cross + Bear: Trials related to power or finances.
- Cross + Star: Hope and faith arising after a period of suffering.

- Cross + Stork: Difficult changes involving necessary sacrifices.
- Cross + Dog: Loyalty tested or sacrifices in a friendship.
- Cross + Tower: Sacrifice related to institutions or hierarchical structures.
- Cross + Garden: Suffering or trials in social or community environments.
- Cross + Mountain: Spiritual obstacle or prolonged karmic test.
- Cross + Path: A difficult decision with spiritual or emotional implications.
- Cross + Rats: Suffering caused by wear or small accumulated losses.
- Cross + Heart: Romantic relationships involving sacrifice or emotional burden.
- Cross + Ring: A commitment that involves responsibility or trials.
- Cross + Book: Trials related to secrets or hidden knowledge.
- Cross + Letter: A message related to trials or sacrifices.
- Cross + Man: A man facing karmic lessons or personal suffering.
- Cross + Woman: A woman dealing with spiritual or emotional burdens.
- Cross + Lily: Peace achieved after significant suffering or trials.
- Cross + Sun: Overcoming trials with success and clarity.
- Cross + Moon: Emotional or spiritual trials related to intuition.

- Cross + Key: A solution that comes after facing a necessary sacrifice.
- Cross + Fish: Sacrifices related to finances or material resources.
- Cross + Anchor: A heavy burden.

"The key to interpretation lies not in the cards themselves, but in the wisdom and creativity you bring to their story."

Note: Image created by Liz Figueroa with AI

INTERPRETATION STRATEGIES FOR NEGATIVE CARDS

CONTROL YOUR EMOTIONS AND PREJUDICES

- *Recognize Personal Perspective*: Before you begin, reflect on how the negative cards make you feel. Do any of them evoke fear, anxiety, or specific memories? Identifying your emotions towards these cards will help you separate your personal experiences from the reading.
- *Neutrality Exercise:* Take a moment to breathe deeply and visualize each card as a neutral symbol, not as something "good" or "bad."

USE THE CONTEXT OF THE QUESTION

Adapt the Interpretations to the Topic: Negative cards do not always have the same meaning.

For example:
- *In love*, the Mountain can indicate emotional distance.
- *In work*, it may represent delays or logistical challenges.
- *Practical Example*: If the Coffin appears in a work-related question, think in terms of "end of a project" or "closing a stage," rather than something strictly negative.

OBSERVE THE POLARITIES

Positive/Negative Balance: Negative cards are often

influenced by adjacent cards. See how positive or neutral cards soften their impact.

Example:

- If the Fox is between the Sun and the Star, it suggests that the strategy will lead to a favorable outcome.
- *Neutral Cards as Bridges*: Learn to use neutral cards (like the Letter or the Book) as transitions between positive and negative cards, adjusting the tone of the reading.

PRACTICE THE "GENERAL APPROACH"

Expand Your Perspective (Zoom Out): Instead of focusing on a single negative card, look at the entire spread to identify the flow of energy and the overall tone.

- *Example:* Clouds + Key + Sun. Although the Clouds suggest confusion, the overall tone is positive because the Key and the Sun ensure clarity and success.

EXPLORE CARDS IN COMBINATIONS

Break Down the Combinations: Analyze each card separately before integrating it into the spread. This helps avoid impulsive interpretations.

Example:

- Snake + Path + Anchor. The Snake suggests obstacles, but the Path shows options, and the Anchor indicates stability after making a decision.

Note Repetitive Combinations: Record frequent combinations and how you've interpreted them in different readings. This creates a "personal dictionary" that you can consult.

AVOID DRAMATIZING NEGATIVE CARDS

Change Your Internal Narrative: Instead of seeing a card as "bad," focus on its practical message.

Example:

- Instead of seeing the Cross as suffering, think in terms of "necessary sacrifice for success."
- *Use Constructive Language:* If reading for others, avoid alarmist phrases. Change "you're going to have problems" to "it's a good time to prepare and anticipate challenges."

KEEP AN OPEN MIND

- *Accept the Unexpected:* Negative cards may have unexpected interpretations. Don't pigeonhole them; allow them to be flexible according to the context.
- *Practical Exercise:* Do readings using only negative cards to explore how they interact with each other and what stories you can build.

PRACTICAL TIPS FOR MASTERING NEGATIVE CARDS

- *Build a Relationship with Each Card*: Take time to study negative cards individually, reflecting on what they represent to you.

- *Do Simulated Readings*: Practice with fictional questions to observe how negative cards affect different topics.
- *Evaluate the Flow of Energy*: Learn to identify transitions and outcomes in spreads where negative cards are central elements.

INTRODUCTION TO THE PRACTICAL EXERCISES

Welcome to the practical exercises section, a crucial part of this ebook designed to help you put into action all the concepts we have explored. Here, you will find 18 exercises that cover fundamental aspects of the negative Lenormand cards, from their traditional meanings to their interaction with positive cards, the use of energy bridges, and strategies for achieving balanced and clear interpretations. These exercises are not just for practice, but also to help you master the art of Lenormand card reading.

These exercises are not just a learning tool, but a focused path to assess your progress. Each exercise will allow you to apply what you have learned practically, helping you strengthen your skills and build confidence in your reading. The answers are provided at the end of each section so you can compare them with your interpretations. You must work honestly and complete the exercises before consulting the answers, as this will allow you to measure your accurate understanding and identify areas where you may improve.

Remember that consistent practice is key to mastering the art of Lenormand. Take your time to reflect on each combination and enjoy the learning process. This space will strengthen your connection with the cards and take your readings to a deeper and more meaningful level. Trust your intuition, it is a powerful tool in Lenormand reading. Give your best effort in each exercise and let your intuition guide you to the right interpretations!

EXERCISES WITH NEGATIVE CARDS

THE CLOUDS

Question:
In a reading about a work project, the combination appears:

Clouds** + **Key** + **Sun

How do you interpret this spread?
a) The project faces initial confusion but has a successful solution.
b) The Key symbolizes problems, and the Sun ensures everything will be positive.
c) There are obstacles with no solution.

THE SNAKE

Question:
In a relationship reading, the following combination arises:

Stork** + **Snake** + **Ring.
What can you deduce?
a) Obstacles in a change, but the commitment remains strong.
b) The relationship faces disloyalties that won't be resolved.
c) The change represented by the Stork is blocked.

THE COFFIN

Question:
For a financial question, the combination appears:

Fish + Coffin + Sun.
What would be your interpretation?

a) Definitive financial losses.
b) Closure of a difficult financial situation, followed by success.
c) A negative end with no clear solution.

THE SCYTHE
Question:
In a health reading, the combination is:

Scythe + Rats + Star.
What message does this convey?

a) A health problem is resolved abruptly, bringing hope.
b) Physical wear with no resolution.
c) A surgery or intervention with no positive results.

THE WHIP
Question:
In a reading about family conflicts, the combination appears:

Whip + Flowers + Tower.
What conclusion can you draw?

a) Emotional conflicts that culminate in reconciliation and strength.
b) Constant problems with no resolution.
c) Inevitable separations within the family environment.

THE FOX

Question:

In a reading about studies, the combination is:

Book + Fox + Clover.

What is the most accurate interpretation?

a) Strategies or precautions in learning that lead to success.
b) Problems in education with no positive results.
c) Lack of necessary information.

THE MOUNTAIN

Question:

In a question about personal progress, the combination appears:

Path + Mountain + Key.

How do you interpret this combination?

a) A significant obstacle that will eventually be overcome.
b) There is no way to progress in this situation.
c) Closed options with no solution.

THE RATS/MICE

Question:

In a reading about the home, the combination appears:

Rats + House + Path.

What does this spread represent?

a) Problems at home leading to an important decision.
b) Losses with no clear solutions.
c) Negative changes at home with no direction.

THE CROSS

Question:

In a reading about spirituality, the combination appears:

Cross + Sun + Child.

What can you deduce?

a) Spiritual sacrifices leading to new beginnings full of hope.
b) Emotional burdens with no resolution.
c) Spiritual problems that aren't progressing.

ANSWER SECTION

- Clouds: a) The project faces initial confusion but has a successful solution.
- Snake: a) Obstacles in a change, but the commitment remains strong.
- Coffin: b) Closure of a difficult financial situation, followed by success.
- Scythe: a) A health problem is resolved abruptly, bringing hope.
- Whip: a) Emotional conflicts that culminate in reconciliation and strength.
- Fox: a) Strategies or precautions in learning that lead to success.
- Mountain: a) A significant obstacle that will eventually be overcome.
- Rats: a) Problems at home leading to an important decision.
- Cross: a) Spiritual sacrifices leading to new beginnings full of hope.

EXERCISES: IDENTIFYING BRIDGES AND POLARITIES

THE CLOUDS: EXPLORING POLARITIES

In a reading about relationships, the combination appears:

Clouds + Star + Flowers

What role do the Clouds play as a bridge between the positive cards?

a) The Clouds indicate initial uncertainty, but the positive cards ensure clarity and harmony.
b) The Clouds dominate the reading, canceling out the positive influence of the other cards.
c) The Clouds have no significant influence in this combination.

THE SNAKE: SOLVING OBSTACLES

In a work reading, the combination arises:

*Snake + Key + Tower***.**

How does the Key act as a bridge in this spread?

a) It resolves the obstacles represented by the Snake and strengthens stability (Tower).
b) It intensifies the problems of the Snake.
c) It has no significant role in this combination.

THE COFFIN: POSITIVE ENDINGS

In a health reading, the combination appears:

Coffin + Sun + Bouquet

How do the positive polarities of the Sun and the Bouquet influence the Coffin?

a) They transform the closure represented by the Coffin into an optimistic and harmonious outcome.
b) The Coffin still dominates with a negative charge.
c) They neutralize the message without generating a clear conclusion.

THE SCYTHE: ABRUPT DECISIONS

In a financial question, the combination appears:

Fish + Scythe + Path.

How does the Path act as a bridge between the Scythe and finances (Fish)?

a) It indicates a new direction after a sudden change.
b) It has no influence on the decision represented by the Scythe.
c) It intensifies financial problems.

THE WHIP: RESOLVING CONFLICTS

In a reading about family conflict, the combination appears:

Whip + Child + Flowers.

How do the positive cards (Child and Flowers) influence the Whip?

a) They soften the conflicts, leading to a harmonious resolution.
b) The conflict remains unresolved.
c) They neutralize the tension without providing clarity.

THE FOX: PRODUCTIVE STRATEGIES

In a reading about studies, the combination appears:

Book + Fox + Star

How do the neutral (Book) and positive (Star) polarities influence the Fox?

a) They transform the strategy of the Fox into a positive path toward success.
b) The Fox maintains its negative charge.
c) The combination has no clear effect.

THE MOUNTAIN: OVERCOMING OBSTACLES

In a question about a personal project, the combination appears:

Mountain + Sun + Path

What does the Sun represent as a bridge in this combination?

a) It provides clarity to overcome the obstacle represented by the Mountain.
b) It neutralizes the message of the Mountain without offering a solution.
c) It intensifies the project's challenge.

THE RATS: CHANGES IN THE HOME

In a reading about moving, the combination appears:

House + Rats + Clover

How does the Clover act as a positive polarity in relation to the Rats?

a) It indicates that the losses will be temporary, and the situation will be resolved soon.
b) The Rats continue to dominate, indicating constant problems.
c) It neutralizes the message without a solution.

THE CROSS: NECESSARY SACRIFICES

In a reading about spiritual growth, the combination appears:

Cross + Key + Sun
What role does the Key play as a bridge in this combination?

a) It provides clarity and a solution to the sacrifices represented by the Cross.
b) It has no significant impact on the sacrifice.
c) It intensifies the weight of the Cross

ANSWER SECTION

- Clouds: a) The Clouds indicate initial uncertainty, but the positive cards ensure clarity and harmony.
- Snake: a) It resolves the obstacles represented by the Snake and strengthens stability (Tower).
- Coffin: a) They transform the closure represented by the Coffin into an optimistic and harmonious outcome.
- Scythe: a) It indicates a new direction after a sudden change.
- Whip: a) They soften the conflicts, leading to a harmonious resolution.
- Fox: a) They transform the strategy of the Fox into a positive path toward success.
- Mountain: a) It provides clarity to overcome the obstacle represented by the Mountain.
- Rats: a) It indicates that the losses will be temporary, and the situation will resolve soon.
- Cross: a) It provides clarity and a solution to the sacrifices represented by the Cross.

SELF-ASSESSMENT: EXPLORING YOUR RELATIONSHIP WITH NEGATIVE CARDS

After exploring this book, this self-assessment will allow you to reflect on your learning process, identify your strengths and areas for improvement, and connect more deeply with the negative Lenormand cards. Answer the questions honestly and use your responses as a guide to continue growing in your practice.

PART 1: PERSONAL CONNECTION WITH THE NEGATIVE CARDS

How did you perceive the negative cards before reading this ebook?
a) I completely avoided them.
b) They intimidated me, but I tried to interpret them.
c) I saw them as necessary tools to understand challenges.

Have you noticed any change in your perspective towards these cards? What specific changes have you observed?

What emotions usually arise when negative cards appear in a reading?

a) Anxiety or fear.
b) Curiosity and analysis.
c) Neutrality and a practical focus.

PART 2: UNDERSTANDING THE CONCEPTS

Do you feel that you now understand better how negative cards interact with positive or neutral cards?
a) Yes, I can now identify how these cards soften or intensify the messages.
b) I have doubts about some specific combinations.
c) I still struggle to interpret them in certain contexts.

What interpretation techniques learned in this ebook have been most useful to you?
a) Observing polarities.
b) Using negative cards as energy bridges.
c) Practicing the general approach instead of focusing only on the negative.

Do you feel more confident in interpreting combinations that include negative cards?
a) Yes, much more.
b) A little more, but I need more practice.
c) I still have insecurities.

PART 3: PRACTICAL APPLICATION

Have you started applying what you have learned in this ebook to your readings?

If so, what changes have you noticed in your interpretations?

What type of combinations with negative cards do you find most challenging?

How would you rate your ability to integrate strategies like observing polarities or interpreting negative cards as transitions?
a) High.
b) Moderate.
c) Low.

PART 4: FINAL REFLECTION

Which negative card do you feel you now understand better and why?

What additional steps will you take to continue improving your relationship with the negative cards?

Do you feel more connected to your Lenormand practice after working with this ebook? Explain your answer.

"In the shadows of the Lenormand lies the wisdom of the unseen—where every challenge holds the power of transformation, and the art of witchcraft unveils the light within the darkness."

Note: Image created by Liz Figueroa with AI

EXPLORING THE NEGATIVE LENORMAND CARDS IN THE CONTEXT OF WITCHCRAFT

The world of witchcraft and cartomancy shares deep roots in the exploration of the occult and the spiritual. While the Lenormand Oracle was not explicitly designed to address witchcraft-related topics, its 36 cards can reflect complex, energetic situations, including those related to spiritual influences or witchcraft workings. It is essential to clarify that in this section, we primarily focus on the negative cards as a tool to explore this topic. However, it's important to note that these are not the only cards that can indicate the presence of spiritual or energetic work.

From my personal experience, I have found that these cards can be powerful allies in identifying potential external influences, understanding how they affect the querent, and most importantly, offering practical guidance and concrete solutions. This section is designed to share not only a logical approach but also my own experiences working with these cards in such a delicate context.

This material is not intended to distort or disrespect authentic practitioners of witchcraft. Instead, it offers an alternative perspective for those seeking to understand this topic from the Lenormand viewpoint, while acknowledging and respecting the deep roots and traditions of witchcraft.

Before performing a specific reading about witchcraft, it is essential to validate the situation using "yes or no" readings to avoid drawing incorrect conclusions or unnecessarily alarming the querent. This type of reading requires experience, maturity, and a deep connection with the oracle. If you decide to work with this approach, I encourage you to do so with compassion and understanding, always remembering that the goal is to help the querent find clarity and solutions.

MY PERSONAL JOURNEY TOWARDS UNDERSTANDING WITCHCRAFT AND LENORMAND

Being from Puerto Rico, I am no stranger to the aspects of witchcraft and the consequences of its use or misuse. As a child, I remember my mother's fascination with Santería and my father's interest in spiritualism, while both faithfully attended Catholic mass every Sunday. This unique upbringing allowed me to grow among three prominent spiritual traditions in my land. I learned to fear them for their opposing sides and to respect them for their positive aspects. However, after years of exposure, I decided to distance myself from these practices to live my life from a less dramatic perspective. Now, I share my personal experiences to educate others on the importance of understanding these traditions.

Although I distanced myself, it does not mean the lessons learned disappeared. I witnessed that I had been a victim of witchcraft during my first marriage, which left deep scars in my life. These experiences taught me not to ignore the potential and consequences of witchcraft. Some might say that witchcraft is merely a cultural belief, a psychological effect. But, in my experience, I have seen that its impact transcends the victim's ignorance, and the damage is real.

In 2016, I faced one of the darkest events of my life. I found myself on the highway, feeling an invisible force pushing me towards suicide. It was a thought that seemed to come from outside of me. I remember pulling over, tears streaming down my face, and pleading with God to help me continue. This was a moment of profound despair, but it was also the beginning of my journey towards healing and understanding.

I began to investigate the cause of this attack. At first, I thought it came from negative people in my environment, those who lurk in the shadows while offering nothing to criticize me. But soon discovered that the source was much closer and more personal. I had recently ended a two-year relationship after discovering, during one of his drunken episodes, that my partner had betrayed me. As the saying goes, "Drunkards don't lie." Shortly after, strange things began happening in my home: dense presences, unpleasant smells, and one day, I even saw a distorted face looking at me through my living room window. I tried cleansing my home in every way possible, but nothing seemed to work.

After the highway incident, I received a call from a fellow tarot reader I had not heard from in a long time. She told me that a woman had come to her office with one of my business cards, which had my photo, asking her to perform a ritual to end my life. My colleague, recognizing me, firmly refused, warning the woman about the consequences of such a dark act. But the woman did not care and left angrily.

When my colleague described the woman, I immediately recognized her: she was my ex-partner's mistress. It was not enough for her to have destroyed my relationship: she also wanted to ensure that I disappeared completely. This realization was a shock, but it also provided a clear motive for the attack. With the help of experts on the subject and a lot of personal work, I overcame this experience. When everything calmed down, I began to reflect: How could I use Lenormand to detect witchcraft, just like it is done with Tarot? I spent months gathering information, asking questions, and consulting with close friends. That is how I developed my technique for this type of reading, which I tested with my students.

Today, many people ask me about these topics and the cards' meanings in the context of witchcraft. Although I avoid talking about it, there are times when I think that it is necessary.

I do not believe in teaching everything, especially on such delicate topics, but I think it is essential to offer an idea of Lenormand's possibilities in this field. One thing I can conclude from my story is that the power of witchcraft is real. It's not just imaginative. If humans, made in the image of a God, are equipped with the power of consciousness and soul, who can deny that this power can also be used to harm others? That is why we need to learn about witchcraft, not to practice it, but to be prepared. If we face such an attack, we will know how to protect ourselves, heal, and regain our balance. Knowledge is our best defense.

HOW TO PERFORM WITCHCRAFT READINGS WITH LENORMAND

Although I do not consider myself an expert in witchcraft, my experience has allowed me to gain knowledge on this topic. However, I often prefer to avoid discussing this subject with my students, as I am unaware of their spiritual preparation or personal motives for using Lenormand in this context.

All the material described in this section should be taken as literary teaching rather than as a practical guide to witchcraft. I intend to share an educational perspective that allows exploration of how negative cards can reflect such energies in reading, always with the utmost respect and within ethical boundaries.

Validate the Consultation Before Starting

Not all consultations related to witchcraft are valid or necessary. As a seeker of spiritual guidance, your role is crucial. Before performing a reading, it's important for you to determine if there are indeed reasons to suspect negative. spiritual influences. One way to do this is through a "yes or no" reading, using specific spreads to represent a clear confirmation or denial. This helps avoid misunderstandings or generating unnecessary fear, putting the power in your hands.

Energetic Preparation of the Reader

Working with witchcraft topics can be emotionally intense and energetically demanding. Before performing any reading, it is crucial for the reader to:

- Perform personal energetic cleansing.
- Set up spiritual protections, such as prayers, candles, or amulets.
- Be emotionally balanced and prepared to handle any outcome.

Structure of the Reading

Spreads specifically designed to explore witchcraft should be clear and focused. A helpful spread might include three cards:

- First card: Represents possible witchcraft or external influence.
- Second card: Shows how it is affecting the querent.
- Third card: Indicates the motivation or intention behind the witchcraft.

Example Spread:
Whip* + *Clouds* + *Snake

- Whip: Confirms the presence of a spiritual conflict or energetic attack.
- Clouds: Reflects the mental or emotional confusion caused in the querent.
- Snake: Reveals that the motivation behind witchcraft is envy or jealousy.

Ethics in Readings
The reader must handle these consultations with care and professionalism, ***avoiding***:

- Making statements that generate unnecessary fear.
- Proposing solutions outside their knowledge or capability.
- Judging the querent or the supposed source of the witchcraft. Instead, offer clarity and guide the querent toward practical and spiritual solutions.

Providing Advice and Solutions
A witchcraft reading is not complete without guidance on how to resolve the situation. This may include:

- Recommendations for energetic cleansing, protection, or proper rituals.
- Suggestions for consulting spiritual experts, if necessary.
- Promoting calmness and confidence in the querent, reminding them that there are always ways to regain control over their energy.

Lenormand, a mirror to the spiritual world, demands care, compassion, and professionalism when used for delicate topics like witchcraft. These readings, when approached with ethics and respect, can be a potent tool for bringing clarity and solutions. As a reader, you play a crucial role as a bridge between the oracle and the querent. Your primary goal is to guide, not to instill fear.

SPREAD TO VALIDATE YES OR NO IN THE PRESENCE OF WITCHCRAFT

Before diving into an analysis of witchcraft, it is essential to confirm whether there is indeed a spiritual or energetic influence present. A three-card spread is ideal for this purpose, as it minimizes the ambiguity that often arises when using five or more cards in this context.

The most common method involves determining the answer based on the majority of the polarities:

- If *the majority* of the cards are **positive**, the answer will be "yes."
- If *the majority* of the cards are **negative**, the answer will be "no."
- If there is a balanced combination of positive, negative, and neutral cards, the answer will be "maybe."

Another approach used by some Lenormand readers is based on the symbols (or inserts) of the cards:

- If *the majority* of the pips are black (♠ spades and ♣ clubs), the answer is "no."
- If *the majority* of the pips are red (♦ diamonds and ♥ hearts), the answer is "yes."

It's important to note that while these 'yes' or 'no' methods are standard, they're not always the best. The Lenormand system is designed to blend cards and interpret them literally, providing a more precise and detailed narrative.

Therefore, it's recommended to use these methods with caution and always. validate them with a literal interpretation of the cards. This combined approach can provide greater clarity and reduce potential misunderstandings, giving you a sense of security and confidence in your readings.

If the answer is "no," the same cards can be used to explore why the suspicion is not related to witchcraft. On the other hand, if the result is "yes," it is recommended to perform a new spread to identify the type of spiritual influence present. This could be a positive influence, such as a guardian angel, or a negative one, such as a malevolent spirit.

MY PERSONAL TECHNIQUE FOR DETECTING WITCHCRAFT WITH LENORMAND

Once the presence of witchcraft has been validated through a 'yes or no' spread, a simple yet powerful technique where the cards are used to answer a specific question, it is essential to delve deeper into the nature of the spiritual influence detected. My technique is based on a three-card linear spread, read from left to right, with a clear focus on identifying the key aspects of witchcraft: its nature, impact on the querent, and the motivation or purpose behind it.

The final position in this spread (position 3) is not just a card, but a gateway to understanding the deeper layers of the situation. It plays a significant role, as it reveals the perpetrator's motivation or goal towards the victim and the final result they seek with the ritual. In addition to the linear reading, I use the mirror reading method to maximize the information, combining the first card with the last one to uncover additional details.

Structure of the Spread and Meaning of the Positions

In this technique, each card has a specific role:

- **First card**: Describes witchcraft or the energy being channeled.
- **Second card:** Represents how this energy directly affects the querent.
- **Third card:** Reveals the motivation, the goal of the ritual, or the perpetrator's desire towards the victim.

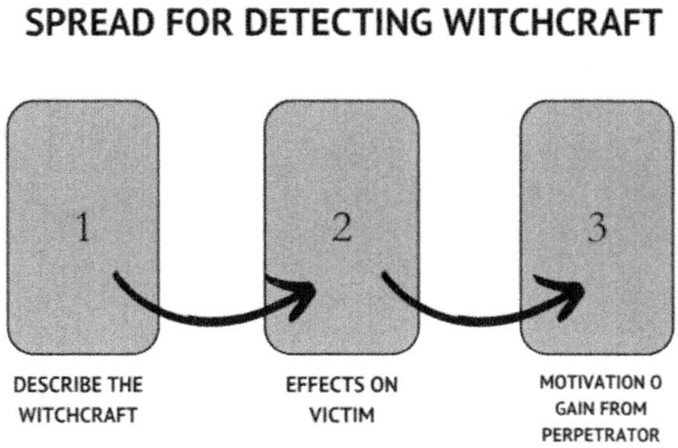

Fig. 4 Witchcraft detection spread by Liz Figueroa

Example of Spread and Analysis

Cards: **Whip + Clouds + Snake**

1. First card (**Whip**): Indicates witchcraft that is related to conflicts, intended to cause aggression or constant tension.

2. Second card (**Clouds**): Reflects the impact on the querent, who may be suffering from mental confusion, distress, or difficulty making clear decisions due to the ritual.

3. Third card (**Snake**): Points out that the perpetrator seeks to manipulate the victim through envy or desires to create an environment of chaos that results in isolation or a loss of self-confidence.

Detailed Linear Reading:

Whip + Clouds: Suggests that the initial intention is to provoke disputes that cloud the victim's judgment.
Clouds + Snake: Indicates that these doubts and confusion are designed to facilitate the perpetrator's goal, which is to sow distrust or cause a significant diversion in the querent's life.

Mirror Reading:

Whip + Snake: Combined, these suggest a calculated and persistent attack, designed to keep the victim in a constant state of vulnerability and under control.

RECOMMENDATIONS FOR HANDLING THE SPREAD

Avoid Hasty Interpretations:
Always analyze the cards calmly and take the time to understand how they relate to one another.

Confirm with Additional Readings:
If you have doubts about the interpretation, perform a complementary spread to validate the results.

Maintain an Ethical Approach:
As a reader, your responsibility is to guide the querent toward practical and constructive solutions, avoiding generating unnecessary fear.

PERSONAL REFLECTION

This personal technique is designed to provide clarity and depth when exploring witchcraft topics in Lenormand. Using linear and mirror readings ensures that important details are not overlooked. By assigning specific meanings to the card positions, we guarantee a structured and objective analysis, instilling confidence and assurance in your readings.

Always approach this spread with respect and sensitivity, ensuring you offer the querent a clear view of what is happening and possible steps to manage it. Remember, their understanding is key, so be responsible and considerate in your approach.

MEANINGS OF THE NEGATIVE CARDS IN THE CONTEXT OF WITCHCRAFT

This section delves into how negative cards can reflect witchcraft rituals, highlighting both their traditional meanings and interpretations within the context of Latin American witchcraft. Additionally, practical solutions to counteract these influences are presented, helping readers approach these situations with clarity and empowerment.

THE CLOUDS
General Concept: Represents confusion or spiritual blockage caused by negative energies.

Example:
Persistent doubts, psychic attacks, or the influence of third parties that sow uncertainty.

Latin American Witchcraft
Witchcraft is represented by the clouds. The Clouds symbolize rituals performed with smoke, such as fumigations or herbs, to cause mental confusion, madness, or even illnesses affecting the head. It may also involve rituals with skull-shaped candles, energies of the four elements manipulated with dirt or ashes from the deceased, which are made to be ingested by the victim.

Possible Solution

- Use a seven-wick grave work candle.
- Perform fumigations to cleanse the environment.
- Implement personal spiritual protections.

THE SNAKE
General Concept: Symbolizes manipulation or envy that may have led to an act of witchcraft.

Example:
Obstacles in the path caused by people with negative intentions.

Latin American Witchcraft
Witchcraft represented by: The Snake, is associated with binding work, envy, and severing any kind of bond. It can also involve channeling dark beings from the lower astral, black magic, or satanic rituals, often performed with ropes, cords, or bindings.

Possible Solution

- Prayers of liberation and protection.
- Perform a black magic cutting ritual with St. Cyprian. Proceed with a ritual to undo bindings.

THE COFFIN
General Concept: Indicates the end of something, but with a purpose of transformation.

Example:
Closure of a stage or situation that leads to a new opportunity.

Latin American Witchcraft
Witchcraft represented by The Coffin reflects rituals that use closed elements such as boxes, coffin-shaped candles, or burials in cemeteries. These practices

seek to torment the person, destroy their health, and cause calamities such as inexplicable sadness, phobias, and misfortunes. It may also include rituals with bones or the invocation of spirits at wakes.

Possible Solution

- Perform a tomb work ritual for black magic.
- Fumigate the space and take baths with bitter herbs.
- Pray to strong saints for protection and cleanse negative energies.

THE SCYTHE
General Concept: Marks an abrupt cut that transforms a stagnant situation.

Example:
A radical decision or an event that changes the course of events.

Latin American Witchcraft
Witchcraft represented by: The Scythe represents extreme cutting rituals, including those intended to cause accidents or death. These practices are often performed in cemeteries or with sharp tools such as needles or pins, usually linked to Santa Muerte or wandering spirits.

Possible Solution
- Consult an experienced witch who works with entities to cut these energies.

THE WHIP
General Concept: Represents repetitive tensions or conflicts that lead to a resolution.

Example:
Constant conflicts that, over time, strengthen the situation.

Latin American Witchcraft
Witchcraft represented by: The Whip reflects extreme revenge rituals performed by powerful black witches. These aim to provoke violence, destruction, fear, and physical or astral torment, using metal tools or invoking entities from the lower astral.

Possible Solution
- Perform a black magic cutting ritual immediately. Use St. Benedict's cross as protection.
- Pray the cross prayer before sleeping.

THE FOX
General Concept: Signals cunning or caution needed to handle a difficult situation.

Example:
Using strategic intelligence to overcome a challenge.

Latin American Witchcraft
Witchcraft is represented by the Fox, which symbolizes rituals often performed by women to get what they want at the expense of others. These rituals are lighter but aim to cause envy and jealousy and are usually performed at night using animals or simple tools.

Possible Solution
- Turn the black magic back.
- Create a protection capsule against envy.

THE MOUNTAIN
General Concept: Indicates obstacles that require patience and effort to overcome.

Example:
An important barrier that can be overcome with persistence.

Latin American Witchcraft
Witchcraft represented by: The Mountain reflects blocking work in all areas: economic, love, family, and health. These rituals aim to create obstacles and total ruin, using elements like salt, cemetery dirt, or any object designed to prevent someone's progress.

Possible Solution
- Perform an unblock or reversal of magic ritual.
- Clean the place where a suspicious object was found with holy water and ammonia, without touching it with your hands.

THE RATS
General Concept: Represents losses or wear that require immediate attention.

Example:
An economic or emotional wear process.

Latin American Witchcraft
Witchcraft, represented by The Rats, is associated with powerful black magic aimed at causing illness, destroying finances, or creating chaos in the home. These rituals can involve contaminated food, pests like worms or flies, and bad smells to affect the victim.

Possible Solution

- Cut the black magic with a specific ritual.
- Completely clean the house with holy water and vinegar.
- Fumigate with incense, myrrh, copal, or benzoin, and take baths with bitter herbs.

THE CROSS

General Concept: Signals necessary sacrifices to achieve a spiritual or material goal.

Example:
A difficult challenge that, when overcome, leads to significant growth.

Latin American Witchcraft

Witchcraft represented by The Cross symbolizes intense black magic work performed on cemeteries or crosses. These rituals include burying photos; salt crosses on doors to curse, and powerful prayers designed to cause ruin or suffering.

Possible Solution

- Perform a banishment of black magic and a tomb work ritual.
- Take purging baths with bitter herbs and coarse salt for 7 days.
- Make a novena to St. Benedict with 9 purple candles, praying his prayer and complementary prayers.

FINAL WORDS: A NEW BEGINNING WITH THE NEGATIVE CARDS

You have reached the end of this section, but your journey with the Lenormand cards is just beginning. The once intimidating negative cards now hold profound significance, serving as portals to self-discovery and transformation. With the tools and insights provided, you are now equipped to face these cards with courage, decipher their messages, and use them as guiding lights in your readings.

Remember, Lenormand is an ever-evolving art, and you are an integral part of that journey. Each spread, question, and reflection deepen your growth as both a reader and a person. Embrace curiosity and allow yourself moments of pause when needed, knowing that every step forward adds to your understanding and mastery.

Thank you for letting me be part of your journey. I encourage you to share your experiences, challenges, and progress with the community and with me. This is not the end but the start of a more meaningful relationship with your deck. The cards have much more to reveal, and I look forward to seeing how far your path takes you. With love and admiration for your dedication,

Liz Figueroa

Your teacher and eternal student of Lenormand

About the Author: Elizabeth (Liz) Figueroa

Born in Puerto Rico and living in the United States since 1999, Liz Figueroa has devoted over 30 years to the art of cartomancy. Her passion for divination began at a young age, fueled by a fascination with life's mysteries and a desire to uncover deeper truths.

Specializing in tools like Tarot, the Lenormand Oracle, and the Kipper Oracle, Liz has been sharing her expertise with students worldwide since 2014, inspiring them to unlock their potential in card interpretation. Liz's approach to teaching is enriched by her diverse skills, including Kipper Oracle reading, Reiki (Levels 1 and 2), charm casting, and Mediumship. Her unique blend of traditional methods and spiritual insight creates a learning experience that is both practical and transformative. Liz's warm, relatable style makes her teachings accessible and meaningful, empowering students to connect with the cards on a deeper level.

A former member of the Tarot Association USA and an active participant in The International Lenormand Network, Liz has shared her knowledge at international conferences and events across Europe and the USA. Known for her innovative approach and global perspective, she has become a respected voice in the esoteric community, particularly within the Spanish-speaking world.

Liz's mission is simple yet profound: to inspire her students to see the cards as not just tools for divination but as gateways to reflection, growth, and self-discovery.

About This English Edition

This book is the English adaptation of the original Spanish edition titled ***Cartas Negativas Oráculo Lenormand: Desafíos, Enseñanzas y Nuevas Perspectivas*** by Liz Figueroa Lenormand, which can also be found on Amazon.com in softcover format.

As a special addition to this English version, readers are granted access to a QR code that leads to a **downloadable PDF** of the ***Steampunk Lenormand deck by Liz Figueroa.*** This deck is designed to be printed and used for personal exploration and practice, complementing the teachings in this book.

flipbook QR Code

Connect with Liz Figueroa Lenormand

For updates, visual demonstrations, and additional resources, you can find me across various social platforms under the name ***Liz Figueroa Lenormand***:

- Facebook
- Instagram
- Telegram
- X (formerly Twitter)
- Pinterest
- Tumblr,
- Threads

Additionally, I have a **YouTube channel** dedicated to visual demonstrations and tutorials to further enhance your understanding of the Lenormand system. Join the community and explore the world of Lenormand with me!

For more information on Lenormand decks made by Liz Figueroa:

ETSY.COM: ***PDF Format deck of cards***: Visit my Etsy Store under "Liz Figueroa Lenormand https://www.etsy.com/shop/LizFigueroaLenormand?ref=seller-platform-mcnav

Shopify.com: ***PDF Format deck of cards*****:** **www.mundomisticolizfigueroa.com**

Makeplayingcards.com: ***Physical Deck of Cards*****:** Visit my store: https://www.makeplayingcards.com/sell/lizfigueroalenormand

¡ Your Feedback Matters!
Thank you for reading this book. Your opinion means the world to me and helps other readers discover this work. Once the book is live on Amazon, you'll be able to leave a review directly. I'd truly appreciate it if you could take a moment to share your thoughts about how this book has supported your journey with Lenormand.

Looking for the Spanish Version?
Great news! This book is also available in Spanish under the title [Insert Spanish Title]. If you or someone you know would benefit from reading it in Spanish, you can find it on Amazon. Simply scan the QR code below.

Printed in Dunstable, United Kingdom

66374861R00087